THE NEXT VALLEY OVER

THE NEXT VALLEY OVER

AN ANGLER'S PROGRESS

CHARLES GAINES

Foreword by Terry McDonell,

Editor, *Men's Journal*

Crown Publishers

New York

Published by Crown Publishers, New York, New York.
Member of the Crown Publishing Group.

Random House, Inc. New York, Toronto, London, Sydney, Auckland
www.randomhouse.com

CROWN is a trademark and the Crown colophon is a registered trademark of
Random House, Inc.

The following stories were originally published in *Men's Journal:* "The Cajun
Road" (November 1998), "Fatboys Lonesome Traveling Fishing-Guide Blues"
(May/June 1993), "Fishing for Grace" (November 1996), and "The Next Valley
Over" (June/July 1995). Copyright © 1993, 1994, 1996, 1998 by Men's Journal
Company, L.P. All rights reserved. Reprinted by permission.

Printed in the United States of America

Design by Leonard Henderson

Library of Congress Cataloging-in-Publication Data
Gaines, Charles, 1942–
The next valley over : an angler's progress / by Charles Gaines — 1st ed.
1. Fishing—Anecdotes. 2. Gaines, Charles, 1942– I. Title.
SH441.G33   2000
799.1'2—dc21   99–049508

ISBN 0-609-60539-9

10 9 8 7 6 5 4 3 2 1

First Edition

To Donald Francis Burke, and
to Monte, Justin, and Chris Burke.

And the end of all our exploring
Will be to arrive where we started
And know the place for the first time.

—T.S. ELIOT, *Four Quartets*

CONTENTS

A C K N O W L E D G M E N T S

The author wishes to express his gratitude to Terry McDonell, John Rasmus, Sid Evans, John Atwood, Chris Buckley, and Patrick Cook for the space in their magazines that made possible many of the piscatorial peregrinations recounted herein.

F I S H I N G ' S

I N N E R G A M E

by Terry McDonell, Editor, *Men's Journal*

Charles Gaines is a handsome man. I mention this not to flatter or embarrass him, but to set you straight about his handicaps, which are numerous and important within the context of this new book of his. Most great fishermen "win ugly," which means that they simply will not be denied their chosen fish on any particular day. Gaines is more complicated. The perfect cast has been his forever and he is a confident man, yet he has told me on more than one occasion that his own image in a morning mirror can spook him so badly as to send him to the Herradura before breakfast: *Face, I know not who you are but I am going to shave you.* Something like that. Charles Gaines is not crazy; but rather so deeply eccentric and graceful in his fishing life as to pass from time to time into what his friend, the great sporting writer Vance Bourjaily, calls "the trance of instinct." This is when Gaines' life is most vivid, most engaged, most hilarious, most sacred. This is what he writes about in *The Next Valley Over*, and this is why all the fishing is so important.

Nothing about writing is ever easy, except maybe the idea of it. The literature of fishing is flush these days with middle-aged white guys, most of whom are a little too quick to mention the time they enjoyed a drink with Charles Gaines at Ballynahinch Castle in Connemara or wherever. They've all been to a great lodge somewhere: Wilson's on the Miramichi, Seven Spirits Bay, Arroyo Verde, or maybe even Perry Munro's smallmouth spike camp on the Black River—but Gaines has been to all of them. As journalists like to brag, he's done the reporting. With all appropriate respect for Izaak Walton and the great Roderick Haig-Brown, this is the book Merriwether Lewis would have written about fishing if he were a better writer and as good a fisherman as Gaines, which he most certainly was not. The truth is that Gaines has been leading his own private Corps of Discovery for a very long time—"gone sprinting bushwhack between valleys." In this light, it almost begins to make sense that the amortization of the market value of the fish he catches some years has to run to $500 a pound. Ergo, if you fish and read on a level of sophistication above dynamiting gar, Gaines is your writer, although he has done that too. In fact, as I start to write a sentence about Gaines being an explorer at the shining bottom of his soul, that bull wacko of all saltwater fishermen, Ted Williams, jumps into my head swatting line-drive triples off the center field wall at Fenway. In the end, it's all about art.

And fish. Charles Gaines knows his fish. He knows, for example, that most saltwater gamefish live "like Greek playboys, following pleasure and abundance from one sunny spot to the next," and that of the roughly thirty thousand species of fish that inhabit the earth, the tarpon is arguably, pound for pound, the gamest. He imagines them "coming in from the deep water at night, on a rising tide, under a waxing three-quarter moon, sensing the landmarks, the certain and particular characteristics of the place, and then registering pleasure or relief from the instincts switching off that brought them to it—like getting off a train late at night, and recognizing, just from the way the air feels, a place you are happy to have traveled a long way to return to." Gaines is especially good on tarpon, but his knowledge from big game down to smallmouth bass is astounding.

Charles Gaines' choices in life—to become a writer; to test himself physically; to sacrifice for his craft; and ultimately to spend an extraordinary amount of time on the water—are on the fault line of talent and ambition that fractures American literature. Hemingway and Zane Grey are in this book, not just in anecdote but in spirit. But so too are Jimmy Buffett, Bayou Pon Pon, and Dion and the Belmonts. Likewise you will find the "Hegel of fishing guides" and any number of hard cases and sporting media entrepreneurs. And in the middle always is Gaines, somehow playing Huck and Tom at the same time— shooting out street lights with his BB gun at age nine or hooking a thousand-pound black marlin "rising as suddenly and menacingly as a revolution" thirty years later. This is an outlaw book in so many ways.

As you get to know Gaines, you wind up visiting him much more than he will ever visit you. In the twenty-five years we have known each other, we have had dinner perhaps five times in New York City where I live; and I have gone to wherever I could find him more than 20 times. Charles lives and plays in interesting places. That beautiful farm in New Hampshire for so many years, the property in the Abacos, his high-tech Swiss-Family-Robinson hideout on the Nova Scotia coast, Guatemala, Africa, the deepest possible Alabama South. The secret truth is that when you visit Charles, you don't actually have to fish, but you had better be hungry for the physical details of his world, the tastes and smells and colors that wash over him like rain.

I have notes, lists of reasons to read this book, starting with the jaw-dropping recognition of self—if you've ever caught a fish you'll see yourself in this book. Then there is the lesson that good times should be orchestrated and not left to the uncertainties of chance. Gaines plans ahead, even for the accidental side of his life. More interesting, I think, is that he wants you to understand that there is no sadder story than a life of small regrets. He wants to move you with his perfect pitch and surgical detail, then he wants you to put the book down and go out looking for places where you may find "a precise sufficiency of methods of purpose, and an effortless and invisible rightness that seems to ride the air and fall over you as diffusely as sunlight, leaving you with the dangerous sense that the time you spend there is what life is meant to be like." He's trying to teach you something: fishing's inner game. Study hard.

When Gaines' literary agent, the ever-patient Dan Green, was asked what the introduction to *The Next Valley Over* should be about he replied hilariously that he wanted only one question answered: Why all the fishing? My answer is that Gaines is an animist who believes in the ritual of fishing—the reflective silences of the tiny trout stream and the "non-stop wet dream of fun in a faraway place catching huge fish to loud music with a buzz on." No flock-tending rules and conventions for Charles Gaines. It is all, as he likes to put it, "how it should be." You have to admire a man who does what he wants and writes like an angel, a man who in his own words has been "caught and released." God, I love this book.

New York City
1/20/2000

PART ONE

Striking the Tent

I T IS APRIL IN ALABAMA, 1957. THE DOGWOODS ARE vivid and suggestive on the hillsides surrounding the lake, and the bass and bluegills are on the beds. Fifteen years old and more wise-ass by far than I have any need to be, I am in the bow of an aluminum johnboat. My father sits in the stern, running the electric motor. He is fifty-one, in his prime. He is happy and open this afternoon as he always is when he is fishing, particularly on this lake. The lake, which my mother has named Tadpole, is less than an hour from our home in Birmingham. My father and a couple of other men have owned it for two years. It is his haven from his job and other demons, and it is our haven from the worst of each other.

My father is working the shoreline with a yellow popping bug, covering every good lie with his jerky but efficient flycasting, catching (so far; we have just gotten to the lake, and dusk, the best time for bass, is a couple of hours away) lots of bluegills the size of your hand. He whoops every time he hooks a fish, and cackles as he plays the bluegills' tight, furious circlings. This annoys me. The whooping and cackling seem out of proportion to the hooking and catching of such small, common fish. I slouch and dream in the bow, as is usually my wont for the first half hour or so of our trips out here. I think of the River Dee in Scotland, about which I have recently read, and the salmon that live in it, and I scroll the surface of the water with the tip of my Orvis Superfine fly rod. The honey-colored cane rod was my father's Christmas gift to me a few months before, and it annoys him that I am using it now so carelessly, to so little end, but he won't say anything about it—not here.

He does say, "You'd better throw your worm in the water, Skip. Fishing's not a spectator sport, buddy." He says this often, and he means life as much as he does fishing, long before that sentiment became a bumper sticker. I work out some line and wonder how a man his age, a man who has caught marlin and other huge fish in places I dream of going to, who I've seen catch bonefish in the Bahamas and brown trout in Montana, could possibly get so worked up over the little bluegills here in Lake Tadpole. Maybe, I think, he's faking it. For me, maybe. But my father never fakes anything, and I know that.

We both cast to a log angling into the water off the bank. "Fish in your half of the boat, Skip," says my father. A bluegill sucks in his popper with the sound they make, like blowing a kiss. My father whoops and cackles, his face glistening with joy. "There's plenty of lake here for both of us."

◆　　　◆　　　◆

We always had home water to come back to, to catch bass and bluegills and to get along, but from the git-go, fishing to me meant traveling to fish.

My father loved to travel, as long as he could do it in style and make fishing the major if not the only point. In the manner of the forties and fifties, he and my mother usually traveled without children, but they would take me and my sister along with them once or twice a year and on a two-week vacation out west every summer. Neither my mother nor my sister was interested in fishing. That left me, and I became his fishing partner on these family trips—to Florida and the Bahamas,

Wisconsin, Maine, Mexico, the Rocky Mountains—from the time I was old enough to hold a rod.

I believe that the majority of anglers who travel to fish are by nature either pastoralists or nomads. My father was a pastoralist, a pure lodge man, who liked to go someplace and hole up there for the duration of the trip, getting to know a particular piece of water in intimate detail over a period of time while having the same table for dinner every night. I, on the other hand, was a born nomad. I can remember, in my teens, lying awake at night in dude-ranch cabins in Montana, fantasizing about stealing the keys to the rented car parked outside. I would take my waders, a rod, and a pack full of bananas and hot dogs, and I would depart that single valley to which Fate and my father's vacation choice had confined me, and drive north to the next valley over—and then to the next, and the next, fishing each as I went until I ran out of Montana. Then I thought—if Lynne Dye wasn't already writing me passionate entreaties to come home to Alabama and marry her—I might just continue on into Canada, and then into whatever place was north of Canada.

But though I was from the beginning, in my soul and dreams anyway, a fishing nomad, I did acquire early on from my father his pastoralist appreciation for fishing lodges and camps. In fact, while he was unforgivingly discriminating about them, I have rarely met a fishing lodge I didn't like (though certainly I have liked some much better than others). I believe this is because for as far back as my memory goes I have associated fishing lodges with vacations, with my father's big, hearty, entertaining presence, and with unspoken but unbreakable truces between the two of us as long as we were in one: with fun, peace, and good humor, in other words. And to this day I'm happy for a night or two in lodges that serve up nothing much more than that, along with edible food.

But I am happier still (and can ignore my nomadic urgings for longer) in the lodges and camps where a lot of small, well-engineered parts cause the place to come together as reassuringly as the closing of a Mercedes's door. This is not the same as luxury, though luxury can be one of those parts. I think of the old Walker's Cay Club in the Abacos, which my father and I used to visit. It had giant palmetto roaches in the bedrooms and a small shark in the swimming pool, but it could stir a delicious contentment in you that left you pining for the place weeks after you'd left it. I think of two or three fly-out lodges in Alaska, where the first thing you wonder on stepping out of a floatplane is "How on earth could this place have *gotten* here?" and of the similarly astonishing and deeply luxurious Seven Spirits Bay Lodge on Australia's remote Coburg Peninsula. Of Bahía Pez Vela in Costa Rica, and Fins and Feathers in Guatemala, and Tropic Star in Panama. Of the cottage camp above the lake at Quillen in Argentine Patagonia. Of Ballynahinch Castle in Connemara, Old River Lodge and Wilson's on the Miramichi River in New Brunswick, Camp Bonaventure in the Gaspé, and Perry Munro's smallmouth spike camp in Nova Scotia. Of New Zealand's eight great fishing lodges, and of the incomparable Arroyo Verde in Argentina—which is made to stand in this volume for all the others. What these places have in common, in addition to very good fishing, is a precise sufficiency of methods to purpose, and an effortless and invisible rightness that seems to ride the air and fall over you as diffusely as sunlight, leaving you with the dangerous sense that the time you spend there is what life is meant to be like.

You can grow accustomed to good guiding in the same hazardous way; and though guides and charter captains, like lodges, are usually more of a pastoralist's enthusiasm than a true nomad's, I developed a lifetime appreciation for them, too, on fishing trips with my father. Before I could drive a car I learned to fly-fish for tarpon in skiffs off of Islamorada, Florida, from men like George Hommel and Jack Brothers—and if that won't give you the hots for good guiding, nothing will.

Since then I have had the good fortune to fish with lots of talented guides, many of whom have become friends, and frankly I couldn't live with myself if I didn't mention a few of them here: my journalism partner, Tom Montgomery, a character in many of these stories, who is as complete a guide as he is a photographer; Bob Butler, Paul Bruun, and Gary "the Wedge" Wilmot, who brings a wolverine's intensity to the job; Captain Hook Hamlin, Peter Wright, and Jody Bright in big game; the non-pareil Kiwi trout guides, among them Peter Church, Tony Entwhistle, Peter Carty, Tony Hayes, Hugh McDowell, Vern Brabant; in shallow salt water, Marty Sawyer, Hank Brown, Jeffrey Cardenas, the inimitable Danny Ayo, the irascible and opinionated Tommy Robinson. Personally, I happen to prize strong opinion and irascibility in a fishing guide, along with a flair for providing lunches, a sense of humor, and the determination and imagination to do whatever has to be done to catch fish. And no one I know owns more of those qualities or puts them together more vividly than A.J. DeRosa, whose wit and wisdom, as the sort of Hegel of fishing guides, is chronicled here and forms for me a canon for the uncompromising, idiosyncratic commitment that the best guides make to their work.

❖　　❖　　❖

I got married when I was twenty-one and moved away from Alabama, and I didn't fish at Lake Tadpole or with my father very often after that for the next twenty years. But I did go fishing during that time—halfheartedly and mostly out of habit at first, then later with a rediscovered and increasingly monomaniacal passion. In my thirties I began traveling to fish and to write for various magazines about that travel, and I have been lucky enough to continue to carry that particular license to steal right up to the present. The stories in this volume come from nearly thirty years of having a look at the next valley over. I took my enthusiasm for good lodges and guides with me, but increasingly during that time I became the singleminded nomad with a rod I had dreamed of being as a teenager until, almost totally blind from Next-Valley Fever, I wandered off the edge of my own map.

Nowadays I travel less, I fish often at Lake Tadpole again, and I fancy that I can see a sort of shape or design to my life as a fisherman. I have tried to arrange the stories in this volume into sections that correspond with that design and illustrate it, without regard to the chronology in which they were written.

For some time I wanted to write a novel that would be a sort of angling *Pilgrim's Progress*, with a very slow learner for a hero. Now that I realize I have largely lived that story, I have no more desire to write it. Real progress began for me somewhere in my mid-thirties with the realization that no matter however else I might be benighted, I would no longer, ever, be one of the poor souls referred to in this quote from Thoreau that I copied off of A.J. DeRosa's dashboard:

MANY MEN GO FISHING ALL THEIR LIVES WITHOUT
KNOWING THAT IT IS NOT FISH THEY ARE AFTER.

From that moment on, I knew it was really dreams I was after. My dreams then all had big fish in them. They had me solving difficult angling problems and beating odds on far-off waters, and living the life of Riley while I was at it. But no matter; at least I had thrown my worm in the water.

WOKE AT 3:45 A.M. BEFORE THE ALARM CLOCK WENT OFF and sat up in the little bed, my head full of Tasmanian dreams: wind, merino sheep in a white opium poppy field, cruising brown trout with foreign accents.

I turned off the clock so it wouldn't wake my five sleeping teammates, and dressed—pile long underwear and lots of wool, waders and felt-soled boots, a raincoat. My old fishing vest, with its familiar bulges and clinkings, went on last. I clipped a net with a retractable handle to my wader belt, stuffed a knapsack with a camera, extra clothes, and two or three of the miniature bottles of Dewar's scotch they had welcomed us with the night before, and went out to the narrow hallway to pick out two rods.

There were nineteen of them standing there, each humming with its own specific action inside a sleek aluminum tube. Made of precisely layered and tapered cones of graphite and boron-graphite, with high-tech initials like IM-6, IMX, RP III, and HLS-19 designating a modulus of elasticity here, a taper or tensile strength there, some of these rods were prototypes, and all of them were state-of-the-high-present-art of fly-rod making.

Tyler Palmer, a flamboyant American ski racer in the 1970s, told me once that when he stepped into his bindings before a race he could hear his skis humming to him of how they wanted to perform. Fly rods, like skis, are things to moon over, bridges between dreams of action and action itself, and I cannot even look at one without imagining its particular character in my hand.

I picked out a kelly green 5-weight with a soft tip in case the wind was down, and a fast, prototype 8-weight, with a reel seat of cocabolla wood and a half-wells grip, in case it wasn't: the former hummed of settling a dry fly onto the nose of a sleeping cherub; the latter of pushing sixty feet of line into God's own sneeze.

Outside the Team U.S.A. cottage was a calm, early summer night in November under the Southern Cross. It was not yet four-fifteen, but Bronte Park was active. Lights were on in the other team cottages, and other anglers on the early morning shift were trudging in waders through the eucalyptus trees toward the bus that waited for us in front of the main building. I gave my name to the brisk Australian official standing by the bus and was given an identification tag to pin on my vest and a scorecard. Two or three men were already sitting by themselves on the bus, looking sleepily out of windows into the velvety Tasmanian dark. Naomi and Wynonna Judd sang to us over the intercom.

I put my knapsack and rods in the overhead rack and sat down behind Tony Entwhistle, the legendary New Zealand trout guide and a member of the New Zealand team. Like most Kiwis, Tony loves to talk, but this morning he was preoccupied. He gave me a floating nymph he had had some luck with in the practice sessions, and I hooked it into the fly pad on my vest.

"Will you be over this summer?" Tony asked.

"In March or April, I think."

"Good. We'll take a few days off and fish for fun."

Tony and I have had a number of unforgettable days

together on New Zealand rivers. One particularly magical one on the Sabine the year before tempted me right then to start bridging memory into thoughts of fishing four or five months in the future, but I was already dream-engaged.

Over the next few minutes the bus filled with fly-rod anglers from seventeen countries. They climbed aboard, nodding to each other, put their rods and knapsacks into the rack above them, and silently took their seats, like commuters in fishing vests. At four-thirty on the dot, the bus pulled out for London Lakes. Over the intercom, Willie Nelson opened the Eighth Annual World Fly Fishing Championship with "Whiskey River."

My "controller" at the first of the morning's two beats was a dignified forester named David. It was David's job to watch me fish for three hours, to make sure I didn't cheat or stray outside the boundaries of my beat, and to measure, record, and release any trout I caught. It was my job simply to fish for Old Glory.

David and I reached the shore of Lake Samuel at five-fifteen. There was no wind, so I strung up the 5-weight, tied on a No. 14 Red-Tag Beetle in the growing light, and walked down to the edge of the water. My beat was three hundred yards of shoreline, with a flagged stake at either end separating me from other anglers. There was a shallow grassy cove to the left, which was perfect for spotting cruising trout to cast to, and two hundred yards of rocky drop-off to the right for blind casting if no fish showed in the cove. David asked me what I did for a living. I told him I wrote, and also sent people around the world on dream fishing trips like this one.

"This is a competition," he corrected me. I didn't feel like arguing.

Two musk ducks splashed thirty yards out in the calm water. In the eucalyptus woods behind us a kookaburra kicked off its maniacal morning chuckling, a sort of birdsong version of P.J. O'Rourke on the subject of Democrats.

There were red and green parrots in those woods, too, and wombats and spiny anteaters. And somewhere in there, his mean little teeth clicking, a Tasmanian devil was finishing off a road-killed wallaby. In the grasses, we had been told, were tiger snakes, a quick and certain end to your fishing day.

And in the *water*, of course—in the deep black water of London Lakes and the emerald coves I was to fish later at Bronte and Little Pine Lagoons—swimming below the ducks and swans and platypuses and through my dreams for months before coming here and for weeks after leaving, were the big, wary Tasmanian brown trout.

My friend Vance Bourjaily has written truly that bird shooting is a sojourn back into the trance of instinct, and in that trance "if a bird falls, it is like being able to bring back a token from a dream."

And so it is with fishing: the ancient saratoga in the rainforest rivers of Cape York, the black bass of New Guinea, the Nile perch and mahseer of Africa and the bonefish of Christmas Island are all—like cow-pond bluegills to a farm boy—tokens, a rod away from dreams. It's the dreams that give them weight and value.

At 5:28 I slid a pair of amber Polaroid glasses onto my nose, stepped into a lake in the central highlands of Tasmania, opened my ears, and looked for references. Fish are fish everywhere, but everywhere they have different accents. The best you can do is listen carefully and look for references. Fly-fishing is a game of skill, but more than that it is a relaxation of normal attentions and a drift into instinct as absorbing and renewing as sleep.

False-cast, the green rod hummed of leaders straightening

two feet off the water and flies dropping as quietly as wishes. On the dawn air was a faint, sleepy scent of eucalyptus burning—a faint haze in the still air, a hush.

"It's five-thirty," said David. "You're fishing, mate."

I straightened a cast into the haze, two feet above the water, and let it fall.

HEART OF THE

OLIVE

THE HUGHES 500 HELICOPTER FOLLOWS THE FISHY RAPID-and-pool sequences of the upper Tongariro River, passing over cultivated fields, with the three great snow-capped volcanoes of the Taupo basin looming to the east. Within fifteen minutes you're over the beech-forested, roadless foothills of the Kaimanawa mountain range, then twisting up the valley of your river for the day, a legendary North Island, New Zealand, bush river, its turquoise runs and deep green pools glinting with sun and promise.

The chopper sweeps up the valley like skiing powder turns, scattering trout from their lies in the river. After a while it hovers, circles downward, lets you and Tony Hayes out on a gravel bar, and lifts off, making a little whirlwind of sand on the bar.

You hold your hat and watch it climb out of the steep, beech-dense gorge. Then it is gone and there is no sound other than the river, the trilling of a bell bird and a waterfall's distant hiss upstream. You stand and let the remoteness soak into you. Only thirty minutes after having breakfasted on venison sausage at Tony's glorious Tongariro Lodge, you are now a three-day walk from the nearest road or house, in a place visited by no more than ten or twelve humans a year.

You string a rod. Somewhere upstream, maybe in the next pool, lies the biggest trout you have ever seen—ready to rise out of the dark pool of imagination and into your astonished reality. All you have to do then is catch it.

◆　　　◆　　　◆

One of the favorite recipes of the great eighteenth-century French epicure Grimod de La Reynière was called "A Roast Without Equal": "an olive stuffed with capers and anchovies inside a figpecker inside an ortolan inside a lark inside a thrush inside a quail wrapped in a vine leaf inside a lapwing inside a fat pullet inside a pheasant inside a wild goose inside a turkey inside a bustard, the whole thing to be cooked in a pot with onions, carrots, ham, celery, lard, spices and herbs, hermetically sealed over a low fire for twenty-four hours."

La Reynière describes the result as "the quintessence of plains, forests, swamps, and the best poultry yard." And Alexandre Dumas noted that "at the end, one threw away everything but the olive, the apex of quintessence."

Think of that lark as fly-fishing clear rivers for big trout; the ortolan as having those rivers all to yourself; and the figpecker as having those rivers to yourself in heartbreakingly beautiful country. The olive, then—that apex of the quintessence of fly-fishing for trout—can be nothing other than helicopter fly-fishing in New Zealand. The elements of that quintessential experience, the "plains, forests, swamps, and the best poultry yard," if you will, that give this olive its particular, ineffable flavor, are solitude, some of the world's loveliest riverscapes, and sight fishing in air-clear water for big, difficult fish.

Difficulty is the caper at the heart of the olive.

◆　　　◆　　　◆

You and Tony walk the bank slowly and look for fish, staying low and in the trees whenever you can to break your outlines.

You find the first one, a brown trout of around seven pounds, in the second run above the bar where the chopper dropped you off. You watch him for a while and see from the occasional white flash of his opening mouth that he is feeding lazily on nymphs. You check your knots, kneel at the water's edge some thirty feet behind the fish, false-cast out of his cone of sight to measure the cast, then chance your throw, as the French say.

If it is right, the fish will not see the fly line. Twelve feet of transparent leader tapered to four pounds breaking strength will drop the fly three feet upstream of the trout's nose, and the nymph will sink at the right speed and float without drift (because you have techniqued out the drift; if you haven't, you can forget the fish) down the fish's feeding lane and into that white-flashing mouth. Very often, however, your throw is not quite right, and these fish are unforgiving. This time your first cast doesn't get deep enough. Spotting for you from the bank, Tony says the second is too far left. On the third, the trout is history.

A quarter of a mile upstream, a rainbow trout hangs in the pellucid, turquoise center of a deep pool that looks like it ought to have Tarzan's Jane emerging from it. Water tinkles into it from a steep, miniature waterfall; ferns trail in its calm edges. The fish is suspended, feeding piggishly in the foam line—a single fish you could die happily after catching—but *there is no way to cast to him*. You discuss it in whispers, crouching in the brush that here grows so close to the river's edge there is no room for a right-handed back-cast. There is a small chance you can cover the fish, you decide, if you wade out below the tail of the pool and can manage to squeeze sixty feet out of a *back-handed* cast with a weighted nymph: the caper at the heart of the olive.

You do it; the huge rainbow inhales the fly, and fifteen minutes later you have run, following the fish, almost all the way back to the bar where the chopper let you out. Finally, Tony nets the trout—an honest nine and a half pounds by the scale in his net handle—and you hold it as carefully as you would a newborn for a picture, then slip it back into the tugging current.

You are now forty-five minutes into your day. Upstream you have seven hours of fishing ahead of you and four or five rough miles. You will see at least four fish today that are over ten pounds, and one giant of maybe fourteen; and you know that there are even bigger fish than that holding in this remote, mysterious, blue-green water. The biggest and most difficult resident river trout in the world, in fact, live in this river, hidden like dreams until they rise up to meet you. Unless you are spending the night on the river, the chopper will pick you up near dusk and take you back to a hot shower, a drink, smoked trout canapés, a baron of New Zealand lamb, a big native Cabernet, and a sumptuous bed.

After a day or two of this, any other trout fishing you may have done will seem like daytime television.

◆   ◆   ◆

Tony Hayes has eight or nine rivers he choppers clients into from Tongariro Lodge. Three of these are trophy rivers, where the fish will average seven pounds and an angler on any given day will almost positively cast to a trout of ten pounds or more. On others of his helicopter rivers the fish are smaller, averaging around four pounds, but a good angler might catch twenty of these in a day.

From Simon Dickie's splendid Poronui Ranch, also on the North Island, clients can be choppered in to one of five peerless bush rivers. On one of these, Simon, Tom Montgomery, and I spotted fourteen fish over seven pounds in a half-day's fishing. Fifteen minutes of helicopter time from the banks of this river put you in the Jacuzzi on the deck at Poronui with a drink in your hand watching pretty Simone grill the venison steaks or paradise duck breasts.

There are similar delights to be had on the South Island. Ray Grubb's Lake Brunner Lodge near Hokitiki, Dick Fraser's Cedar Lodge near Wanaka, Mick Mason's Motueka River Lodge and Bob Haswell's Rotoroa Lodge, both near Nelson, all offer guided helicopter access to pristine bush rivers during the day, and world-class wining, dining, and lodging at night.

And for people who don't want lodge-based fishing, there are a very select number of top independent guides on both islands who specialize in chopper fishing. One of these, the redoubtable Tony Entwhistle from Nelson, has probably done more helicopter fishing with clients than anyone in New Zealand. He believes that chopper fishing has less negative impact on the fragile bush environment than many hike-in fishing trips, which he also guides into some of the same remote areas; he believes, too, that helicopter fishing is all about mystery and dream, and he wants to write a book about it someday called *No Footprints in the Sand*.

My first New Zealand helicopter fishing experience was in 1984 with another of those independent guides. Vern Brabant took my wife and me up to a South Island river whose name sounds like "Whockamui," where we camped in an old deer-culler's shack. For three perfect days we fished to the biggest and most discriminating trout I had ever seen in an untellably beautiful setting. At night Vern would butterfly a trout, plank it on twigs, and run it up the chimney on a branch to smoke while we sat around the fire eating smoked oysters and then fried lamb chops, drinking good Scotch out of tin cups, and listening to the "more-pork" birds and the possums howling in the bush. It would have taken more strength than I have not to become addicted.

New Zealand's backcountry trout can haunt you as no other fish can do, and the rivers they inhabit can come to possess a part of your imagination and memory. Hughie McDowell from Rotorua is one of the North Island's best and most experienced helicopter fishing guides. He is also one of the most charming men alive and he owns a poet's soul. Once on a chopper camping trip to a particularly poignant river whose name sounds like "Myaroa," Hughie and I took a break from fishing to sit on a couple of boulders and have a taste of single malt from the silver flask his wife, "Knuckles," had given him. We tasted and sat, tasted and sat, listening to the mesmerizing chatter of the river.

"You know," said Hughie, "whenever I'm in a bus station, or Los Angeles, someplace I really hate, *doing* something I really hate, all I have to do is say the word 'Myaroa' and I'm here. It's like stepping into a dream."

On one of the elegant upstairs walls of the Motueka River Lodge there is a gouache done by a young New Zealand artist named Peter Jewett, who is wise enough, reportedly, to do nothing with his time but paint and fish. This picture is a portrait of the olive: A man stands in a wild stream, his back to us, sunlight on his hat, his right arm, the tip of his rod, and his fly line. He stands on a bar of silver-dollar-sized stones, white, yellow, red, and russet, exactly as they are in the real river. There is a thin plume of silver broken water downstream of his legs, exactly as there should be, and pinpoints of light on the rippled water's surface.

In front of the man the bar drops onto a white sand bottom; beyond that the water deepens to green and then almost to black against the rock face of the bank.

Silhouetted against the white sand is a huge, dark trout. The angler's rod is bowed, either in lifting the line for a cast or in striking this fish—this great, once-in-a-lifetime fish, emerged from the black run by the rock face and now here, visible against the white sand for a single moment of possibility. For a moment, dream has become a difficult, one-time opportunity, and there is late sunlight on the thin line running from the mind of this man to the fish, either in offering or in contact.

The name of the stream in the picture sounds like "Rarimea."

FAT BOY'S LONESOME
FISHING GUIDE BLUES

I'd better gather up my tackle
And wind a little hackle,
I've got another fishing job tomorrow morning.
It's five hundred miles from here,
Just got time for one short beer.
Fishing with these geeks can sure get boring.

—FROM "FAT BOY'S LONESOME TRAVELING
FISHING GUIDE BLUES," BY A.J. DeROSA, SUNG
TO THE TUNE OF RED STEAGAL'S "RODEO BLUES"

IT IS AROUND TEN-THIRTY ON A BEAUTIFUL MONTANA MORN-
ing. It is windless, the sky is clear, and the temperature is rising
along a steep western spring trajectory that has already taken it
well into the sixties from near freezing at first light, and will carry
it into the nineties by midafternoon. A.J. DeRosa, sole proprietor
of "Fat Boy Fishing, Custom Fly-Fishing Trips Throughout the
Intermountain West"; Tom Montgomery, fishing guide, photographer, and longtime DeRosa fan and friend; and I are standing
hip-deep in eastern Montana's Bighorn River, fishing a particularly trouty-looking run. A.J.'s old wooden drift boat is anchored
by the bank, with his black Lab, Caladonia, snoozing in the bow.

We have been on the river since sunup. We were the first boat to put in this morning below the dam at Fort Smith, but the customary Bighorn hordes are out now and the river is choked with drift boats and anglers in a recurring nightmare for A.J., one he had to learn to live with.

As it happens, many of these anglers don't know much about what they are doing. For example, after about five minutes of nymphing the run I hook a fat rainbow that jumps garishly several times and attracts the attention of an angler casting thirty yards upstream of us, close to the minimum polite distance. The man watches me fight the fish, net it—a dark, nicely colored henfish, it is, of about five pounds—and release it. Then he strolls down the bank and begins fishing no more then twenty feet from me, angling his casts downstream to cover the same water the rainbow had come from. He even looks over and offers us all a sweet, dumb grin.

Standing by his boat, A.J. says loudly, "The amazing thing about this river is that guys will just come right into your hole and start fishing. I mean, sure, some of them are just *natural idiots and don't know what the hell they're doing, but they should learn.*" Just then the unfortunate fisherman hooks a trout. He glances guiltily over his shoulder at us, at A.J. staring holes through him, and the fish—very possibly the only one he will hook all day—breaks off. The man sighs, obviously relieved, and reels in his line. As he trudges ashore, he says, pathetically, "I'm sorry I'm in your hole. I've never fished here before. I didn't know."

The geek knows now, taught by the stern schoolmaster of the Bighorn; what he *doesn't* know is that he got off lightly. Others on this river have suffered much harsher lessons in fishing etiquette from A.J. DeRosa. Like the three guys who once floated right over a pod of feeding fish that he was casting a dry fly to, then parked their boat and began fishing *between* him and Tom Montgomery. Montgomery is small but feisty. He stomped over to the three men and began dressing them down, but when A.J. walked over he was oddly calm, almost conciliatory. Tom couldn't believe it. The three guys agreed unpleasantly to walk upstream out of sight to fish. A few minutes later, Tom watched A.J. fish down to their boat, dawdle by it for a while, then casually fish his way down to Tom. "Tom," he said sunnily. "Don't get mad. Get even." And he held up the plug from the interlopers' boat.

"I take fishing personally," is A.J.'s comment on this story.

◆　　　◆　　　◆

With a year-old degree in business administration from the University of Detroit, Anthony John DeRosa drove out west looking for a ski bum's life in 1972. Like many another aspiring ski bum, he settled in Jackson Hole, Wyoming, and has stayed there, more or less, ever since. Within two years he was guiding fishermen on the Snake River for a local outfitter during the summer and fall, and working as a ski patrolman during the winter. Now, eighteen years later, at forty-four, he still hasn't found a better way to split his time and sort of earn a living. And that degree in business administration is now what it was when he first got it: a teat on a boar.

There are fishing guides and there are fishing guides: lazy ones, hardworking ones; good, bad, and so-so ones; charmers and louts. Take it from someone who has fished with most of the identified species, as a client what you should want most in a person you pay to take you fishing is the same thing you should want in a bird dog: a slobbering, breakneck passion for what he or she does.

It should be added that people, fishing guides and otherwise, with such passion tend to be a little idiosyncratic, better kept in the kennel than in the house—a little maverick, if you will. And in fact a whole subcategory of fishing guides of this stripe exists. You can find these hungry-eyed, unhousebroken types on charter boats along the Great Barrier Reef and in skiffs in the Keys, working the fly-out lodges of Alaska, the flats in Belize, and the salmon rivers of Labrador. Anywhere sports plunk down cold cash to be put over fish, you can find some guy who has severely bent his life over going fishing for a living and would happily bend another one in the same way as long as he can have someone in the bow to talk to and buy the beer. Sure, they're a little demanding, maybe, and they might get you in a bar fight or two; they can't be trusted to order the best Calvados, and they rarely if ever come all turned out in crisp khakis the way the guides in the magazines do; but, trust me, these are the guides whose boats you want to be in—whether you enjoy the experience or not.

If there was a Westminster Show for such guides, A.J. DeRosa might win Best of Breed. He pays three hundred dollars a month for rent in Jackson Hole. He owns one-third of a dilapidated trailer; an orange '76 propane-fueled van with a cracked windshield, a sign on the dash quoting Thoreau, and a license plate that says "Fat"; a fifteen-year old, six-hundred-dollar wooden Keith Steele drift boat with trailer; the sleepy black Lab, Caladonia; some skis, waders, and fishing tackle; and that's about it.

"There are two ways of avoiding the middle-class American trap," he says. "You can make a ton of dough and rise above it, or you can drop right out of the bottom. There are two leisure classes in this country, and I'm in one of them. My clients are in the other. That's why we are natural collaborators." This is distilled passionate/maverick fishing-guide philosophy. And so is this: "Very few people realize that you can do exactly whatever it is you want to do."

A.J. likes to ski, but mostly what he has wanted to do since he came out west is fish and take people fishing. He has guided in Alaska, and in 1979 he and a girl named Patty Reilly went down to Patagonia to fishing-bum around, fell in love with that wild, dusty place, and went back the following season to start a guiding business that lasted four years. Otherwise, A.J.'s guiding turf has been and remains the entire "intermountain West."

The great majority of trout guides guide on one river, or maybe two or three, all within easy day-trip distance from their wives and mortgages. But there's a small group of road-loving guides in the West like A.J.—unmarried, unmortgaged, unregenerate—who guide wherever they want to be, hitting the West's great trout rivers as they come hot in a movable feast from the beginning of the season to the end. The Green in Utah; the Snake and New Fork in Wyoming; New Mexico's San Juan; Idaho's Henry's Fork and South Fork; the Madison, Bighorn, Big Hole, Missouri, and Yellowstone in Montana are just a few of these waters, and ones that nobody will care if I name.

A typical ten-day gig for A.J. might consist of meeting a client (probably one of his two dozen or so regulars) at the airport in Billings, fishing the Bighorn for three days, driving a day for two days' fishing on the Yellowstone or in the park, then over to the Big Hole for three days before dropping off the trout-sated sport in Bozeman for his flight back east. From this and from guiding his home-water Snake River in August and September—for a total of some eighty days over five or six months of dusty driving, trailering and untrailering his boat, making lunches, tying leader knots, and taking flies out of trout lips—A.J. *grosses* around fifteen thousand dollars.

Every once in a while he envies the guides who stay on one stream, who guide more days and drive fewer (and he can congratulate the "very heavy wiring in their brains" that allows them to go up and down the same piece of water like a yo-yo day in and day out for the reward, if they are lucky and good, of becoming, finally, the "deans" of their streams), but not very often. Winter is for being in one place. Summer is for moving and the trout-bum, Plains Indian mentality: go where the fishing is good and follow it around, don't leave too much of yourself anywhere, smoke what you can't eat and take it with you.

"Sure, I could've done something else, but everybody pays a price for what they do. We pay a price, and the $200,000-a-year guys we guide pay a price. We're giving them a little piece of heaven for a few days and then they go back to their rat mazes. They give us a little piece of heaven when they lay a nice tip on us and we can go buy a case of good beer, and not have to drink Schmidt's. Drinking Schmidt's is the price we pay."

And then there are the rivers themselves—coming back into them each year one at a time, like into old friends' houses, some better kept than others . . .

> *He's been fishing really bad*
> *And he lost the good ones that he had,*
> *Then he hooks a hog that should've been the clincher.*
> *He smiles a silly grin,*
> *And says, "I broke him off again."*
> *And they don't ever leave no tip for an eleven-incher.*

We go off the river for a couple of hours in midafternoon and back onto it at five-thirty to fish until dark. Just before we take out around two, A.J. and I find a couple of not-very-big brown trout regularly sipping something off the surface in a difficult spot, a spot of floating weed to hang up your fly on every cast and of conflicting currents to ruin your drift over the fish. We fish to these browns for an hour, both of us, taking turns, going to lighter and lighter leader tippets, putting on every fly we can think of, including A.J.'s standby ant—and the two browns disdain to notice us, like a couple of secretaries turning up their noses at whistling hardhats.

A.J. is still in a good mood over this when we start fishing again, but his mood starts to fade when we get a look at our company for the evening fishing. The river is covered upstream and down with drift boats, more of them by far than A.J. and Tom have ever seen this early in the season. Among them, moreover, is a flotilla of ten to fifteen little single-man pontoon boats, horrible little sky-blue, high-tech cheapos that belong in a pond at Disneyland with kids in them, their owners chatting and whooping back and forth, fishing and hollering and drifting inexpertly all over A.J.'s precious Bighorn.

Which was, before the crowds, arguably North America's finest trout river: twelve miles of blue-ribbon water below Yellowtail Dam, floating at a cool, constant temperature. The high pH that the Bighorn gets from its limestone substrata and a high aquatic mineral content encourage vast, fertile weed beds that are fast-food restaurants for trout, and the river is home to more (nearly seven thousand) and bigger wild trout per mile than any river in the continental United States. A large part of it that flows within a Crow Indian reservation was only opened to non-Indian fishing in 1981. For a number of years after that, the river was an uncrowded trouting paradise. A.J.'s first year on the Bighorn was '82, and he's been back every year since. For years here he could show his clients some of the highest-quality trout fishing in the world; now they still catch fish, but what he shows them, too often, is a river full of blue toy boats.

On the bank we drink a tin cup or two of bourbon, smoke stogies, and cook lamb chops, waiting for an evening rise of fish that doesn't happen. A.J.'s first choice for a place to fish this evening was taken, and so were his second and third. He stirs the fire with a stick and watches one of the blue boats float by backwards. "You can see now why the Worm has to be blown up," he sighs.

The Worm is an eight-foot-by-thirty-five-foot 1942 Nashua trailer. A.J. and two guide friends bought it for seven hundred dollars sight unseen from a Mexican in 1983 and lived in it for five or six years, whenever they were guiding on the Bighorn. In its heyday the Worm was parked down at Cottonwoods Campground, where most of the other itinerant Bighorn guides stay, and a lot of life came and went through it in the mid- and late eighties—a lot of partying, a lot of wild duck and Cabernet dinners. Now it is parked in a friend's backyard, dilapidated and unused, a sort of mini-museum of the good days on the Bighorn. The two guides who bought it with A.J. are now both working on second families: one is a business-man, the other a schoolteacher.

These days A.J. stays in George Kelly's house. He can see the Worm from the porch, and occasionally he will walk over and take someone through it. On the trailer's front are painted the words for fishing bums in Spanish, *Los Vagabondos de Pesca;* on the back is a flamingo; and on most of the door-side is the Worm's namesake art—a painting of a mess of writhing night-crawlers spilling out of a tin can: bigger-than-life trout bait. Inside the trailer there are cartoons, news clips, and photos of llamas stuck to the walls. A clipped headline says, "Armpit Skin Used to Make Tongue"; another, from the *Wall Street Journal,* says, "To Many Sportsmen, Flies Are Not Pests But Alluring Objects."

Also pinned to a wall is a poster announcing

THE SEVENTH ANNUAL BOAT-NIGGERS' BALL
KOTTONWOODS KOUNTRY KLUB
FORT SMITH, MONTANA
*"G'wine to row all night,
G'wine to row all day,
De Bighorn River be 12 miles long,
Oh de do da day . . ."*

By the bed is a copy of John Gierach's *Trout Bum*. In the Worm's living room is a fly-tying bench with a sign over it asking, "Who Farted?" There is a calendar of pinup girls from 1981, old fly-tying dubbing, mule deer antlers, mesquite wood chips, shotgun shells, and mourning dove decoys. The little outlived home is pungent with impiousness, with the itinerant, male-bonded, partying, ass-kicking, up-yours life that used to carry on in it. Visiting it, says A.J., makes him feel like Chuck Berry taking reporters through the old Flexible bus he used to tour in—a little sad, but also like grinning when he looks at the bed and remembers all the good times different people had there.

The Worm was a boy's club, a hangout, a crack in the rocks to get away from the posse at a time when A.J. and his two trail-ermates were still young enough to have options real enough to make them feel righteous in refusing them; when "Who Farted?" was the question of the day; when there were damned few overequipped anglers and no little blue pontoon boats on the river; and when clients came to experience the river, not just to catch the thirty fish a day the fly-fishing magazines started telling them they had *every right* to catch. Now the Worm is none of those things, it is abundantly clear that everybody farted, and A.J.'s buddies finally took what options they still had and went south, leaving him just about the last of the original boat niggers at the Ball, looking disconsolately around the middle of a trailer that no longer makes any sense, with nothing left to do but blow it up.

◆ ◆ ◆

Now if I can just hang on
Through the Big Hole and the Yellowstone,
I'm sure to have some fun come late October.
I'll take Caladonia out,
We'll shoot some ducks and kill some trout,
And thank the Lord another fishing season's over.

The next day, angling to catch a "quality fishing experience" with no toy boats in it, A.J., Tom, and I don't get started until noon and then go downriver to a stretch that is less written about and therefore less populated than the stretches just below the dam. We see only one other boat the rest of the day. The float is through the Crow reservation, and both the water and the landscape are lovely. The day is still and hot, there are nesting mallards and Canada geese to watch, A.J. sings his "Fat Boy's Lonesome Traveling Fishing Guide Blues," and we have good fishing on Wooly Buggers. In short, we catch that quality fishing experience, and keep on catching it all afternoon and evening.

And why are there not more sports with their guides down here catching that same experience with us instead of gridlocking each other up above? It has to do, explains A.J., with the nature of the modern client, the modern guide, and the modern guide-client relationship.

Not too long ago, most of the clients he got were one of two types: old codgers who had spent a lifetime fly-fishing and were smoked in the traditions, the etiquette, the literature, and the essential gentleness of the sport; or younger codgers, new to the sport, who *wanted* to be smoked in all those things at least as much as they wanted to catch fish. These clients never killed trout if you asked them not to; they knew how to put down their rods and watch a mother merganser swim by with a clutch of ducklings; they wouldn't fish another man's water if their Mercedes sedans depended on it; and they preferred to learn things well rather than quickly, and to measure their days more by pleasure and camaraderie than by the number of trout they put in the boat. With these clients, or most of them anyway, it was possible for a guide to really be a Guide—someone sharing a treasure trove of experience, doling it out exactly as it was needed—in how to participate productively and enjoyably in one of the most pleasant pursuits mankind has ever invented for itself.

To be a Guide is to be, as necessary, a drill sergeant and nanny, a psychologist and marriage counselor, an entomologist, chef, storyteller, buddy, and subtle imparter of traditions and ethics. The old kind of clients let you do all that, *wanted* you to do all that. But these new guys, these thirty-year-old geeks with ten-million-dollar companies and hundreds of shiny little devices hung all over their vests that they don't know how to use, these graduates of some three-day fly-fishing school who take their cellular phones in the boat with them and don't have *time* for anything—time to listen, time to watch, time to learn, time to enjoy—all *these* guys want you to do is row the boat, smile and chuckle a lot, and look snappy and neat in your Patagonia gear with maybe a purple bandanna around your neck like some Guide of the Year they saw in *Fly Rod & Reel* magazine. And mostly, of course, they want you to catch a lot of fish for them, no matter how badly they fish; they want to rip as many lips on whatever river they're on as the magazines says Joe Expert did.

Fly-fishing now is big business, and if enough customers want something, they'll get it—including white-bread, cookie-cutter guides. A few years ago, whenever a particular outfitter in Jackson Hole ran out of palatable guides to take out his clients, he would call A.J. A.J. would put on the ugliest clothes he could find, roll his good boat off the trailer and replace it with a filthy, leaky old scow with "Abuse Tours" painted on the side, and take his veep-for-the-day fishing. On one of these standby trips, he somehow neglected to remove from the bow a dead, week-old whitefish he'd been using to train his dog. Unfamiliar, no doubt, with the maverick-guide sense of humor, it took the client *four hours* to ask, "Do we *have* to carry this dead fish along with us?"

Around four o'clock we stop on a shady island to cook supper. A.J. expertly butterflies and smokes two small trout for an appetizer. We pour some whiskey into tin cups, fire up cigars, and he puts on the grill a couple of mallards that have been marinating since yesterday. The river rustles by on either side of us and we lounge under a stand of cottonwoods, feeling the day start to cool and darken toward the evening fishing, which is a magical thing wherever in the world you have it.

On the whole, says A.J., he wouldn't trade his life for anyone's. "It takes a lot of stamina to stay a trout bum. But we have the seasons, and the seasons keep you whole. I look forward to the spring when I'm getting back on rivers, I look forward to grasshopper season in the middle of the summer, and I look forward to the leaves falling when I can put a shotgun in the boat and shoot a few ducks at the end of a day of fishing. I think when you're in tune with the seasons, it's hard to have any kind of regrets. I don't know a single old fishing guide who's bemoaning the fact that he's spent twenty or thirty years guiding . . . To be honest with you, I don't even know how people live in the real world."

He thinks he may guide another ten years or so. Then he'd like to open an Italian deli in Jackson Hole, sell prosciutto, Italian sausages, and roasted peppers, ski, play a little saxophone. And, of course, fish. Because whatever he is or isn't, A.J. DeRosa knows he will *never* be one of those geeks referred to in the Thoreau quote on the dashboard of his van: "Many men go fishing all of their lives without knowing that it is not fish they are after."

> *I've got them "Oh oh no,*
> *I Don't Want to Go*
> *Guide a Geek Again Tomorrow Blues."*
> *Listen to 'em whine*
> *When they tangle up their line,*
> *And I can't even pay my Association dues.*

THE WORLD'S GREATEST FISHING LODGE, PERIOD

I N 1972 THE GREAT BELGIAN FOOD WRITER ROY ANDRIES DE Groot wrote an article for *Playboy* magazine that lovingly proposed the French country restaurant Troisgros as the World's Greatest Restaurant. Describing a meal there of terrine de foie gras, lobster in Calvados sauce, and roasted wild duck, the article made you want to eat the paper it was printed on.

It also made the brave point that in this world of mediocrity and qualification, there are still a few identifiable superlatives around, as well as a few reporters with the discrimination and temerity to name them.

De Groot was a blind nobleman, overweight and gouty, who died by his own hand. His appetites were not easy on him, and he spared himself not at all in their pursuit: in explaining how he was able to identify a single restaurant as being the world's greatest, he estimated that since childhood he had dined in 12,474 restaurants around the world and "as far as I can remember, not one of them was ever as good as Troisgros."

Fishing lodges are to me, more or less, what restaurants were to De Groot—an expensive, outsized, debilitating, and lifetime passion. I have shamelessly squandered time and money at them for over thirty years in most of the fifty states, in nearly thirty countries, and on five continents. From castles in the British Isles to a tin aboriginal shack in the Northern Territories of Australia, anything I hear of that calls itself a fishing lodge gets my attention, and usually, sooner or later, me. I have not yet, perhaps, been quite as ruined by my passion as De Groot was by his, but neither have I yet indulged it for as long. I fully expect to; but for now there is more than enough ruin and indulgence under the bridge for me to paraphrase De Groot with authority: since childhood I have visited a truly shocking number of fishing lodges, and as far as I can remember (allowing here for accumulated ruin to brain cells as De Groot wisely did), not one of them was ever as good as Arroyo Verde.

You can reach Arroyo Verde by driving for about an hour north of the southern Argentina resort city of Bariloche; but the prettier way is the two-hour drive south from San Martín de los Andes. If you have stayed at the Hôtel La Cheminée in San Martín, you will have breakfasted well, and if you leave early the air will be snappy and blue with altitude as you drive out past the lake and up into the Andes. You pass streams becoming great Patagonian rivers—the Caleufú, the Hermoso, the Meliquina—tawny, windswept mountains, sandstone monoliths, and strange, Arizona-like rock outcroppings. Then the road drops over Cordoba Pass into a verdant valley, the valley of the Traful, and onto the ranch property.

The name of the ranch—or estancia, *as they are called in Argentina—is Arroyo Verde. It means "green creek." It might as well mean heaven if you enjoy fly-fishing and the major creature comforts.*

◆　　　◆　　　◆

Ernie Schwiebert is a man who fully enjoys such things. A sort of De Groot of fly-fishing, a well-traveled, sybaritic, and discriminating angler and fishing writer, Schwiebert has called the Traful "the world's greatest landlocked salmon river." He has visited Arroyo Verde to fish that river more than twenty times over the past thirty years.

The Traful is twelve miles long from its headwater lake to where it empties into the dammed head of the Limay River. In addition to landlocked Atlantic salmon, the river holds good populations of brown and rainbow trout, and some brook trout. Most of these fish are large, many of them as large as you can dream a freshwater fish to be. This twelve-mile length of world-class fishery belongs entirely to two brothers—Maurice Larivière, who, with his wife, Meme, owns Arroyo Verde; and Maurice's younger brother Felipe, who owns the estancia La Primavera on the opposite side of the river from Arroyo Verde.* Their father bought the valley in 1934 from an Englishman, who acquired it from the area's first white settler, an American adventurer named Newbury. In addition to the Traful River, this Larivière property (both brothers own other estancias in Argentina, as well as town houses in Buenos Aires) comprises 26,000 regally isolated acres, including a couple of mountain ranges.

Maurice Larivière raises red stag, horses, cattle, and sheep on Arroyo Verde, and for the past five years the estancia has been open from mid-November through mid-April (summer in the southern hemisphere) to paying guests. Like Schwiebert, most of those guests come to Arroyo Verde for the first time to fish, but it is more than the fishing, good as that is, that brings them back year after year.

*Since this story was written, La Primavera has been bought by Ted Turner.

The landscape could be southwestern Montana except for the brilliant red Chilean fireweed called notro *blooming on the hillsides. Wild purple lupine is also in bloom, and a butter-yellow Argentine forsythia. The river winks at you as you follow it for miles, pool after pool playing hard to get. There are doves, ducks, geese, and ibis in the air, and thoroughbred horses and prime English beef cattle in green paddocks. A covey of California quail scatters in front of the Jeep, and hares are everywhere.*

"You like hare?" asks Carlos Sanchez, who has brought you here. "Bueno! Maurice will love to shoot and cook one for you."

The ambience at Arroyo Verde is an andante harmony, a nonchalant but careful balance of sympathetic effects. The main house is generous and handsome, made of logs and glass. The grounds around it are expensively but unobtrusively landscaped with flowers and flowering shrubs, the statue of a deer, a fish-holding casting pond and stream, a stone terrace looking out to the river and the mountains. Fat Labrador puppies sleep in the grass. A cat stretches on a lawn table. There is a small village of outbuildings surrounding the main house—a tack house and barn, a guest cottage, a building holding the generators that provide the lodge with power, and housing for the lodge staff and the gauchos who manage the estancia—all of them well placed, good looking, nothing more than what they need to be. Comely as it is, there is not the slightest pomposity about the look of Arroyo Verde; it simply looks perfectly right.

Inside, your room is large and airy, with French doors opening out onto the lawn. The sheets are monogrammed linen; towels in the big, hand-painted tile bathroom are huge and plush; an antique dressing table is set with silver brushes, and there are good books on the bedside table and good art on the walls. You will learn that any clothes you take off in here will be washed, pressed, and returned without your knowing they've gone.

Lunch is at two: scrambled eggs with local mushrooms, a rare eye of round, sautéed onions and spinach fresh from the garden, a salad, and a bracing bottle of vino tinto.

Can this get any better? you wonder over dessert.

Well, yes. There is a siesta after lunch, and at five o'clock you go out fishing. When you return, just after dark at 10:00 P.M., a white-jacketed man meets you just out of your waders with a glass of single-malt Scotch and a silver tray of smoked trout canapés. After a shower, there is champagne with a fresh Argentine Port Salud and Cole Porter playing in the living room. Supper is borscht with sour cream in Spode bowls, followed by eggplant soufflé and toasted homemade bread, a wonderful Argentina Merlot, and a tart lemon mousse. Then coffee is served around a fire in the living room, and you settle in with a snifter of brandy to look at Maurice's collection of prints and first-edition books, and then to watch a tape.

The tape is of an American Sportsman *segment from the 1960s: the legendary angler Joe Brooks is fishing the Traful River, looking as well fed and happy as you are.*

◆   ◆   ◆

Maurice Larivière is said to be the best roll-caster in Argentina. An elegantly efficient and understated method of delivering a fly when obstruction behind the caster makes normal casting difficult, the roll-cast suits both him and his river. Maurice is a fit sixty-five. He rides one of his thoroughbred horses every day while he is at Arroyo Verde, and he is there all summer long. He favors gaucho boots and *bombachas*, the baggy gaucho trousers, and wide cloth gaucho belts. He speaks perfect French and English, and converses authoritatively and energetically on the American Civil War, horse breeding, Broadway musicals, birds, European history, old prints and rare books, bamboo fly rods, and more birds—all of this often in one evening. His wife, Meme, a Buenos Aires *grande dame*, is not always at the estancia during the summer, and it is likely that Maurice decided to open Arroyo Verde to the public because he so relishes good conversation and the company of fellow anglers.

Long before there were paying clients, there was a good bit of that company here, much of it distinguished: Brooks and Schwiebert, Curt Gowdy, Norman Armour, Pickney Tuck, Charlie Gates. And Dwight Eisenhower. The headwater of the Traful is a breathtakingly clear and blue mountain-ringed lake, forty-five kilometers long, called Lago Traful. Maurice owns three or four miles of it and has, on a point near the river's mouth, a cottage that must be for guest couples who choose to stay there, a mile or two from the main lodge, one of the world's most enchanting places to come to terms. Standing near the cottage and gazing down at dozens of landlocked salmon stacked up at the *boca*, or mouth, of the river, Maurice will tell his guests, "This is where Eisenhower fished. He caught nothing."

That rarely happens on the Traful, though it is not an easy river. Lago Traful was originally stocked between 1903 and 1905 with rainbow, brown, brook, and lake trout, whitefish, and landlocked Atlantic salmon from Sebago Lake in Maine, all of them provided by the U.S. Fish and Wildlife Service. The lake trout and whitefish didn't take, but the others did with a vengeance. One of the things that distinguishes the Traful River as a great fishery is its variety—the presence in it of all three major species of river trout *and* landlocked salmon; another is the average size of the fish caught in the river, which for both trout and salmon would be close to six pounds. That astonishing average weight, and the presence in the river of many fish over fifteen pounds and up to twenty-five, is due largely to a rich, year-round food supply of small crustaceans, called *pancora*, in both the lake and the river. The large average size of the fish is also partially responsible for why the river is not an easy one, since few big wild trout are dumb. Then there is the river itself: it is fast and deep in many places, with challenging wading, and casting circumstances that often demand Maurice's roll-cast. There are good hatches of mayflies and caddisflies on the river in March and April, and in those months the dry-fly fishing can be excellent; but for much of the season the Traful is a wet-fly river, with large streamers, nymphs, and *pancora* patterns producing the best results.

The best fly-fishing is always exacting and demanding of concentration. Part of the great pleasure the sport provides is the satisfaction of solving problems, and the more intricate the problems, the greater the satisfaction. Though there are easy stretches and easy days on the Traful, they do not characterize the river's fishing, and that is as it should be.

Something like this would be more like it: You walk down to a fast glide that is too deep to wade; at the bottom of the glide, a polished black pool eddies out behind a bus-sized boulder. It is into that pool, on as deep a drift as possible, that you want to get your fly. There are dense stands of trees directly behind you and downstream of where you're standing, so you work out lengthening roll-casts into the middle of the fast water. You find you can reach the pool this way, but the fly isn't getting deep enough. After a number of failed solutions, you finally jury-rig a cast straight downstream, parallel to the bank, so that you can get a back-cast, release the fly as far upstream as you can on the back-cast, instantly mend the line, mend again, and *yes*, there is the fly in the pool, deep, and you see the tip of the fly line jerk, and something big comes tight. The fish arrows out of the pool, shaking its head, a rainbow or a salmon over ten pounds, and then splashes down and rips downstream. As you watch the backing disappear off the reel, you realize the next problem that needs solving—to add to your overall satisfaction over Scotch and smoked trout back at the lodge—is how the hell to follow this fish.

◆　　　◆　　　◆

Roy Andries De Groot had his criteria for greatness, and I have mine. He insisted that the reception and service at the World's Greatest Restaurant be flawless; that the dining room be comfortable and attractive but not pretentiously luxurious; and that the food be fresh, perfectly prepared, honest, and surprising. He wanted no affectation anywhere, and wrote in summing up Troisgros that "there had not been the slightest pomposity about the food, the service or the welcome."

By my criteria, any fishing lodge that aspires to superlative status must, of course, have excellent fishing, i.e., demanding angling for an interesting variety of big fish. It must also offer superior creature comforts, emollients both for the body and the mind for that preponderance of time when you are off the water. Moreover, the place should have a breath of effortlessly understated elegance, and the days spent there must have symmetry, excitement, and spiritual comfort to them. Finally, and perhaps most important, those qualities must extend to days not spent fishing for whatever reason, be it weather or whim.

It is an achingly clear, windy day. You and your wife don't feel like fishing. Over the past three days you have fished hard and been rewarded with a good number of the Truful's lovely, problematic fish, and now you are temporarily tired of the tightly focused concentration such fishing demands, and ready to air out a little in this high, fine wind.

At breakfast, Maurice asks if you'd like to ride up into the moun-

tains to look for the giant Andean condors that are the western hemi-sphere's largest flying birds. He tells you he knows where there is a nest and there are usually two adults and a young one nearby.

This superb plan is quickly mounted, and shortly so are you, on good horses with gaucho saddles covered with sheepskins, and riding uphill with Maurice and Carlos, led by the estancia's head gaucho and followed by a pack of rangy, big-jawed puma dogs. Over the next two hours you climb 2,600 feet above the valley, over buttes and tan, stony hillsides, in and out of copses of conifers and false ash. Around one o'clock you stop in a glade of trees by a stream for an asado. *Lying on moss, you drink* vino tinto *out of tin cups and eat hard cheese and estancia-smoked salami while the gaucho builds a fire, banks it, and spits a side of lamb vertically on a wooden stake. He spreads the lamb on the stake with twigs, pours hot Chilean* aji *sauce over it, and pushes the stake into the ground a foot or two from the banked fire.*

When the lamb is done, you will cut as much as you want of the charred, pink meat from the bones and eat it with your hands and wash it down with more vino tinto. *Then, after a siesta on the moss, you will ride up to the cliff face where the condors nest, lead your horses to the edge of the cliff, their hooves clacking and slipping on the stone, and look out over the* estancia *and the Traful snaking out of the deep blue lake and through the valley three thousand feet below. And then, perfectly, the condors will appear, like great black gliders, surfing the wind on twelve-foot wingspans, and the afternoon will seem suddenly crowded with superlatives. Tonight there will be another fine meal and good conversation, and tomorrow there will be fishing again on the Traful . . . And all of that is exactly as it should be at the World's Greatest Fishing Lodge.*

PART TWO

Gone Fishing

As we know, the most impotent dreams are the hardest to shake. In my early forties, my teenage reverie of life as a nonstop fishing road trip returned, fastening onto me like a vampire bat, and in less time, it seemed, than it takes to write this sentence, fishing went from something I simply enjoyed doing and wrote an article about from time to time to a bloodsucking lust. For a while in my life it was all I wanted to do; for a shorter while it was virtually all I did do. Moreover, on the infrequent occasions when I was at home with my family, I became a fishing boor, the kind of seized, one-track enthusiast my wife and I have always avoided: an Ancient Mariner who clutches someone's arm at a cocktail party, fixes him *or* her with a glittering eye, and rants on and on about the North Umpqua or the flats at Los Roques.

I developed an unseemly interest in numbers—how many species of fish I had caught, the number of fish I caught on a particular trip, how many continents I had not yet angled. I wanted to go everywhere in the world where anything that passed for a fish could be caught, and even started a sporting travel company to help me do that. My travel was chronic, stripped down, independent, and swift. I no longer had any time for pastoralist niceties, and I developed the nomad's contempt for comfort and stasis, and for all the little flock-tending rules and conventions that fly-fishing, in particular, seemed increasingly to hang on itself like doodads on a fishing vest.

Neither did I have much time for anyone who didn't appear to me to be putting his life on the line for fishing. I had thrown away my own map and compass for being too slow and gone into a sprinting bushwhack between valleys, and I didn't want anyone with me who couldn't keep up or didn't understand why we were running. I fished a full eight or nine months out of a few of those years. I quit writing books, and then anything at all. I neglected my family, my farm in New Hampshire. I went into what a nineteenth-century psychologist might have called a full swoon over fishing.

On a long-distance call I placed from a phone booth in Tasmania, following two weeks of trout fishing there and in New Zealand, my wife and best friend of twenty-five years offered to quit being both of those things immediately if I didn't come home. Instead, I went off to catch northern bluefin tuna at Tangalooma with Malcolm Florence, then on to Cairns, then on to stand-up fishing for yellowfin off of Lord Howe Island, then on to saratoga and barramundi on the Gulf of Carpentaria. I was gone for three more weeks.

Bad luck tends to stalk this kind of lurching imbalance like a hungry wolf. I have always had my share of angling misadventure and mishap, and have only very rarely been the graced, natural angler—Yeats's "wise and simple" fisherman in gray Connemara cloth—that I would love to be all the time. My father secretly considered me a bit of a Jonah, in fact—a banana on the boat; and many are the times people fishing with me have wondered if my middle name might not be "cold front." But all that comes under the heading of run-of-the-mill bad luck. What I am talking about here, what befell me in the fishing frenzy of my forties, was Joblike angling misfortune. I became a one-man El Niño. Storms of the century followed me around. I started breaking lanterns nearly every time I stood up.

Fishing is casting a petition into the unknown, and the eternal wonder of it is that almost anything could be down there ready to bite: your heart's desire; your worst fear; even something big enough to pull you overboard and catch *you*. Like monks, the best anglers are humble petitioners: subtle, quiet, reverent, forbearing. Their sly, insouciant casts hardly make a dimple on the surface of the mystery, and their lines regularly come tight to fish and also to the gentle things they are really fishing for. These are the anglers on whom Lady Angling Good Fortune perennially smiles. What earns her frowns, I learned firsthand, is to come running up before her like a panting, hairshirted John the Baptist with hubris and a rod and begin heaving bowling balls into the lake. If she is in good temper that day, she might simply ignore you. If not, she might hook you up to your very own Moby Dick.

The Next Valley Over

Nothing seems really to matter, that's the charm of it.
Whether you get away, whether you don't; whether you
arrive at your destination or whether you reach somewhere
else, or whether you never get anywhere at all, you're
always busy and you never do anything in particular; and
when you've done it there's always something else to do . . .

THE WATER RAT, FROM
The Wind in the Willows

JUNE 6. A GOLDEN MORNING. MY SON LATHAM AND I HAVE
Texas-cut French toast and scones with honey-butter at the
Chalet in Last Chance, Idaho, drive over Targhee Pass on the
Continental Divide, and come down into Montana just a few
miles from West Yellowstone. We actually began this trip the day
before, but the trout in the flat, oily, maddening water of the
Henry's Fork across from the Last Chance Lodge & Outfitters
were too picky in their eating habits to deserve being written
about. So we are calling this the first day of the trip—a two-week
road-angling tour of Montana that Tom Montgomery and I have
been talking about taking for years and have finally put together.
For the next thirteen days Tom and I will follow the movable feast

of Montana trout fishing from the southwest corner of the state to the northwest, with various friends and loved ones joining in the merriment for a day or two or longer here and there. We will drive more than 1,600 miles one way and fish nine rivers and a half-dozen lakes and ponds on a kickass, blue-highway, blue-plate-special pure Montana road-angling trip: a little planning, a little serendipity, a few coolers full of beer; staying in forty-dollar-a-night motel rooms and eating your five basic meat groups in diners and bars near midnight when you come off the water; some interesting people met along the way; God's own amount of memorable fishing. And after we have done it, as the Water Rat observed about messing about in boats, there will always be something else to do, and I still won't be inclined to discuss those Henry's Fork trout.

At West Yellowstone, Latham and I, in a rented car, follow Tom Montgomery's trailered South Fork skiff along the absurdly beautiful northwest boundary of Yellowstone Park, then swing west around Hebgen Lake and trace the majestic, trout-rich Madison River north toward Ennis. We have the road virtually to ourselves, and that fact and the chaste greenness of the countryside remind us that we are early, in this first week of June, for a fishing trip to Montana. And while the rewards for being early can be significant—few anglers, uncrowded motels and restaurants, wildflowers, hungry fish—the costs in the wrong year, of high water and miserable weather, can put you out of business. This is a low runoff year, and we should be all right, I think . . . Unless we get a lot of rain.

We scoot through Ennis, then through the endearing Old West hokum of Virginia City and into the tiny town of Laurin, pronounced, for some Montana reason, Loray. We pull into the parking lot of the Vigilante Cafe right at noon and go inside to meet Ken Barrett, a friend from Bozeman who will join us for this afternoon's fishing, and John Sampson. John and his partner Paul Moseley are two of the West's new angling entrepreneurs—young guys with money and brains who love trout fishing and have made it their livelihood and life. After lunch at the Vigilante, we all follow John over to the Ruby River just outside of town, where he and Moseley own and lease eleven miles of water and make some of it available to anglers for a daily rod fee.

The Ruby is a river to get a crush on. Petite and sparkling, with fondleable little curves, purling rips, and winking deeps, you might fight a man who said something ugly about this river in a bar. It also has lots of trout in it, some of them hefty. We wade a little and walk the banks, catching fat browns and rainbows on caddis, beadhead nymphs, and Wooly Buggers. It is leisurely, conversational fishing, framed by the Ruby Mountains to the south and the Tobacco Roots to the north, and as blue-gray clouds boil up over the Tobacco Roots, the willow-sheltered Ruby is an intimately serene place to be. Latham catches his biggest brown trout ever, a twenty-incher. And Ken and I catch up with our long friendship—watch each other catch fish, talk about old junctures, shared friends and pleasures.

We fish until after nine and quit just before dark. Back at the vehicles, Ken and I light up cigars, pull on pile against the wind, and take a draw or two off a long-necked bottle of George Dickel as we break down the rods. Ken is driving back to Bozeman and John back to Laurin. Tom and Latham and I are headed for the Stardust Country Inn in Twin Bridges for the night. I tell Ken about a mutual friend who is said to be starting his own country in the Bahamas. He laughs, his big, tough face creasing, and I think of all the rods I have broken down by cars, road-angling over the years with friends, to laughter and darkness gathering over water.

◆　　◆　　◆

The road from Twin Bridges to Melrose is everything a Montana backroad ought to be: winding, rising and falling, rough, muddy, and cleaving through stunning, empty, tan-green ranching country. Melrose has two parallel streets on either side of a railroad track that runs through the middle of town, which here is two bars, a fly shop, a motel, a secondhand store called Needful Things, and a restaurant called The Water's Edge. The water referred to is the Big Hole River, one of the great trout rivers of the West and the reason we are in Melrose.

Latham, Tom, and I meet John Sampson and Paul Moseley at Phil Smith's Montana Trophy Angler at ten-thirty to arrange for a shuttle for a float on the Big Hole. Phil Smith, Tom tells me, committed suicide last winter. His daughter Georgia now runs the fly shop, which is an extension of her house. The license plate on Georgia's rig outside the shop reads FISHIN' GAL.

"So you like to fish?" I ask her.

"It's my life," she says with no inflection. "My dad got me into it." Tom, who has known Georgia since she was a little girl, calls her "double-tough."

While we are filling out the shuttle forms, a friend of Georgia's drops in to say she is going to Dillon, thirty miles away and the nearest town with stores. The friend asks Georgia if she can bring her anything.

"You can bring me a vanilla latte."

The friend looks at her. "It'll get cold."

"Not if you drive fast," Fishin' Gal tells her.

It is warm and sunny when we put in on the Big Hole at Divide, Latham and I in John's boat and Paul and Tom in Tom's.

The annual hatch on this river of the huge stoneflies known as salmonflies is over, but Latham and I tie on three-inch long Sofa Pillow salmonfly imitations anyway, because they are fun to fish, and start catching nice rainbows on them right away. The Big Hole also holds brown, brook, and cutthroat trout, and one of the largest wild populations of river-dwelling grayling in the United States outside of Alaska. Here in its middle section, it is purposeful, generous water, with deep runs and bouldery pockets for nymphing, and bouncing riffles and flat tailouts and backwaters for dry-fly fishing. Running through pastureland, olive hills, and steep rock cliffs studded with clumps of evergreen, rich with ospreys, herons, bald eagles, and Cooper's hawks, demanding attention to fish it well but not fussily technical, the middle Big Hole has provided me with many memorable floats over the years, and it does so again today.

The young entrepreneur fish-hawks from the Ruby, best friends since the fifth grade, are excellent company, anglers, and guides. The weather goes exhilaratingly from calm, sunny warmth to clouds and rain, then wind and snow showers, to clear and warm again. And we catch fish steadily through the changes. Cows bawl from the banks. The wind rises and falls. The boats float in and out of sun. We cast, mend, watch an osprey, chat and work the fly, and the mayfly pleasures of the day hatch and swarm around us.

A mile or so above Melrose some serious clouds move in spitting and snarling from the south, and we take out in a bruiser sleet and snowstorm that makes me happy for the good hot shower and warm room at the Sportsman's Lodge Motel. John and Paul leave for Laurin, and we are joined at the motel by Tom Bailey, a friend and fishing client of Tom Montgomery's from Aspen and a veteran Montana road-angler. We eat dinner together at The Water's Edge, an unlikely hybrid of backcountry Montana café and New Age coffee bar. It is owned and run by an ex-mercenary soldier named Phil Brissenden and his wife, Carol Perez, an ex-exotic dancer. Here in a town where they still drive cattle down the twin main streets, Phil and Carol serve five kinds of coffee but no alcohol. They have recent bullet holes in the walls, and haddock and king crab on the menu. Phil himself brought us out the appetizer du jour. It was fruit, pickles, squash, tomatoes, and nuts on ice.

On an average of once a year I fall in love with some restaurant for totally eccentric reasons. The Water's Edge, I decide, is my new sweetie.

It snows, sleets, and rains all night, becoming, maybe, the big drop we don't need, and Melrose's two streets are puddled this morning when Latham and I cross them for breakfast back at The Water's Edge. After I had gone to bed the night before, Latham walked over to one of the two bars in town to have a beer and play a dollar's worth of nickels in a poker machine. With twenty cents left he hit a royal flush in clubs and it paid him out *two thousand* nickels. There was a silence in the bar when the machine stopped paying. A cowboy in the bag looked at Latham from the bar and offered the opinion that he was "one lucky sonofabitch." Another bar-sitter suggested that it might be nice if Latham bought the house a drink. He did. It cost him two hundred nickels.

We order hash browns and sage sausage, Montana toast, eggs, and one of the five kinds of coffee from Phil. Latham and I are the only ones in the restaurant, so Phil stands behind the coffee bar and chats. He has a hot dog stand on order, he says. That will free him up for lunch—just hire someone to sell the dogs, and he can shut down the restaurant and go fishing. I ask him what it was like to be a mercenary. He says that it and Vietnam turned him from a spontaneously violent man into someone who could control his anger. Most of the time.

"I still get violent when I see a man mistreat a woman," Phil says. "I'll break a guy's face for that. I don't care if he's seven feet tall, I'll break his face, drag him outside, and let the dogs piss on him. That's all a guy like that is good for." Phil stares at me in the eyes. I chew my sage sausage and nod. "I can't understand guys who don't appreciate women," he says, "the best creation God ever put on this earth. They ought to be someplace where there aren't any women for a while, then they'd learn to appreciate them."

Phil fought for seven countries after Vietnam, and put $250,000 in the bank one year. Then he was in the pool-building business. Then he owned strip clubs in Connecticut. He met Carol in one of his clubs. She was part Puerto Rican, part Indian, and one of the best strippers in the East. Now they are in Melrose with a brightly painted coffee bar/restaurant, getting the cowboys and ranchers used to nuts on ice, king crab and haddock, and appreciating their women.

Montgomery and Bailey have been out since a very cold daybreak, photographing at Lyle Reynolds's fee water on a ten-thousand-acre ranch north of Dillon. Latham and I are to meet them there at ten o'clock. We are a little early, and before they arrive we look over Tom Bailey's custom-built Econoline, road-angling van. It's a nomad fisherman's dream machine. It has a bed, a kitchenette, a closet, a fly-tying table, tubes above the bed for ten fly rods mounted with reels, storage under the bed for more rods, and a TV and VCR for fishing tapes. In this van and a predecessor, Bailey has road-angled the state a dozen times, covering somewhere around fifteen thousand miles since 1983, and he is still finding good new water.

Such as Lyle Reynolds's. Lyle runs Sundown Outfitters in Melrose. He has a deal with the owners of this ranch to bring in a maximum of two anglers a day for a rod fee (plus Lyle's daily guide rate) to fish the three miles of spring creek and four miles of lower Beaverhead River that the ranch controls.

Like them or not, rod fees are a permanent feature on the new face of Western trout fishing. As recently as ten years ago, you could knock on a rancher's door and get permission to fish almost any water that ran through private land. Now the state's blue-ribbon trout water, particularly that with no public access, is as valuable as oil. Much of it has been bought by wealthy individuals and posted, some has been privatized by lodges, and on some you can still get permission to fish—but usually you get it now by handing over a rod fee of up to and sometimes over a hundred dollars a day per person. As with other exchanges in life, sometimes you get a bargain, sometimes you don't. With Lyle Reynolds you get more than your money's worth.

Montgomery and Bailey pack up their cameras and leave for our next river, an hour and a half south of Melrose, and Latham, Lyle, and I fish a one-acre pond full of feisty rainbows. We catch a dozen or so on Wooly Buggers, then drive down to the Lower Beaverhead for the main course. The water is in good shape after all the precipitation the night before, and very fishy looking. Not much bigger than a spring creek here, the river snakes across its broad agricultural valley in wide coils that organize the flow into runs and corner pools. The Ruby Range rears to the east of us, the Pioneers to the west, both hatted with fresh snow. Latham and Lyle and I stroll the banks in and out of cottonwoods and willows, and probe the pools with weighted nymphs. The upper Beaverhead, with its amazing seven hundred fish over twenty inches per mile, its deep, fast current, willow-choked banks, and exacting fishing, is one of my favorite rivers anywhere, but there is nothing relaxing about it. This lower stretch is an idyll. Downriver, Lyle's rod bucks. "A fish in ever' hole," he whoops. There is, in fact, and many of them are whoppers.

Less than three hours later, when Latham and I have to leave to meet up with Montgomery and Bailey, we have caught or lost five fish of twenty inches or better, including one hook-jawed, two-foot old brown that comes unstuck right at Latham's feet. It is exceptional fishing on lovely water, and we tell Lyle we will be back as we take to the road again—Highway 41 south to 15 this time, to somewhere south of Dillon.

◆   ◆   ◆

Tom Bailey is putting his rod into one of the tubes over the bed in the Econoline and taking off his waders. I have come back to my car to get a fly box and am surprised to see him ending his fishing with a couple of hours of daylight left. He has just walked, he says, a couple of miles upriver to a pool where he and one of his best friends fished once. That day, Bailey was hung over and took a nap on the bank while the friend caught two nice fish out of the pool. Bailey had wanted to see the pool again and make a cast into it and remember different road trips with that friend, who was now, I knew, recovering from a serious cancer operation in a hospital in Boston. Bailey had just come from visiting him there. Now he has decided to go home. He is just no good for the rest of this trip, he says, though he hates leaving it, particularly on this river.

After Bailey drives off, I go back to the river, to a series of pools upstream of the bridge where I want to finish my evening's fishing. I watch a muskrat swim the river with some hay in his mouth, and swallows strafe the big bridge pool downstream. The light has gone flat and amber. The ragged white Lima Peaks are to the south; to the east, across a few miles of honey-colored pastureland, is a beautifully crumpled range of hills, sculpted like sand dunes in mauve, tan, and olive. We have been fishing for three hours, since around 4:00 P.M. I have seen a bald eagle, Canada geese, redwing blackbirds, many mallards, sandhill cranes, a stuffy-looking phalarope . . . The river is off-color from two days of rain, but Tom Montgomery, Latham, and I have all caught fish, some of them big, and all of them in beautiful condition. Moreover, this river has caught me. I wade into the dull shine of its current, chance a cast, and think, If this were the river in the last valley over, that would be okay with me.

Eleven miles of the river run through the five-thousand-acre ranch that has been in Debbie Tamcke's family for six generations. A number of rich and powerful people know how good the fishing is in that eleven miles, and have tried to buy the ranch from Debbie's family, offering such attention-getting sums for it that the place's value no longer has anything to do with its cattle-ranching potential. The family is tempted to sell, but they don't want to see the river zipped up and put on a shelf by some absentee-waterlord tycoon, as so much of Montana's best water has been recently.* Debbie thinks about building a lodge on the river, but she and her husband know nothing about the lodge business. In the meantime they charge a daily rod fee, and, as with Lyle Reynolds's operation, the fishing and the river experience on the Tamcke ranch is worth every penny of what you pay for it.

We spend this night and the next on the ranch in a comfortable cabin that the Tamckes rent out at a reasonable cost to

*Since this story was written, this river, too, has been bought and privatized by the ubiquitous Ted Turner.

anglers. Tim Linehan drives up from Idaho, towing his drift boat, to join us for the rest of the trip. And at the end of our second afternoon's fishing on the river, Latham drives the rental car back home to his job and wife in Jackson Hole. Before he does that, he ups his biggest-ever brown, on an afternoon when Tom and Tim and I all have hard-to-forget fishing in cool, nervous weather, the creased and folded sage-colored hills glowing to the east like giant runes, and release a fair number of trout back into the off-colored water, some of them of a size that stays between me and the trout.

After fishing, Tom and Tim and I dine at the Peat Bar in Lima, "Home of the Cook-Your-Own Steak." While enjoying a beverage of your choice at this establishment, you pick any size steak you want from a freezer in the back and throw it on a big grill in the middle of the bar. There are deer heads on the wall; poker machines; a pool table. While you cook your slab of frozen beef, you might strike up a conversation with the two pudgy, good-natured girls at the bar, or one of the startled-looking adolescents at the pool table, or the desultory proprietor of the Peat with his feet on the bar, expounding on why whitetail deer are superior to mule deer: a conversation, perhaps, about the road, since everyone here seems equally a Bedouin.

◆   ◆   ◆

At least once on most road-angling trips the fish will whip you like a rented mule, and that's what the pale Missouri River rainbows did to us yesterday. We drove north up Interstate 15 from the Tamcke ranch through Butte and Helena, just past Wolf Creek to Graham Deacon's Lazy-D Fly Fishing Lodge in Dearborn, arriving at about 3:00 P.M. on a calm, hot, high-pressure afternoon that had all of us, Graham included, looking forward to an easy bite.

An old friend of Tom's, Graham is a big, good-humored red-head from Oregon with a ruddy face and a cheerfully doomed sense that he has sacrificed his life to sport. He runs the Lazy-D from early May through mid-October, then goes back to Oregon to guide and outfit for steelhead and ducks. When he is not fishing for a living, he is fishing for fun, as he was yesterday. With no clients presently in, he had offered to put us up for a couple of nights at his comfortable lodge and to show us some of his water.

The thirty miles of the Missouri that Graham guides on, from Holter Dam to the town of Cascade, is a tailwater that looks and fishes like a hundred-yard-wide spring creek. There is a lot of weed growth, and the water is alkaline and slow, with ornately eddying currents that scroll the surface with glassy, oval boils and meandering foam lines. There were flocks of white pelicans on the river and its islands, and we saw geese, mergansers, goldeneyes, mallards, and a few deer coming to water on our float from around four to nine-thirty. We also saw lots of trout, slurping mayfly duns and caddis, and porpoising for emergers, but we caught damned few of them. In our two boats were three professional trout-fishing guides and a geezer who has been to the trout-fishing picnic himself more than once. On this hot, still, perfect afternoon, with fish rising in pockets all up and down the river, we went to fifteen-foot leaders and 7x tippets, tried PMDs and CDCs, beadheads and emergers, ants, Baetis, sparkle duns, spinners, and soft-hackles . . . and, mostly, we had our butts handed to us.

The late light was beautiful on the rock cliffs, though; the fish we did catch fought and jumped spectacularly; and the soups, huge, fresh salad bar, and creative entrées we ate just before midnight at the Dearborn Inn, just a few steps down the hill from the Lazy-D, won the blue ribbon on this trip for best meal under ten dollars.

Today, of course, is another story. Graham wants us to float the Dearborn, a tributary to the Missouri that only fishes well for about three weeks a year, between its water being either too high or too low. We are here in that window, and grabbing opportunities as they float past you is part of what road-angling is all about, so we put in on the Dearborn around ten o'clock.

It is another hot, clear day, and a long one, as the float covers twenty river miles. Twelve of those miles are in a canyon of steep organ pipes and spires of volcanic rock that matches the better-known Smith River canyon for loveliness and solitude. Wild pink roses grow in crevices in the rock cliffs, and swallows wheel in and out of nests there. The river is a glacial blue green, making up into a couple of interesting rapids, choppy runs, and dark, slick corner pools that butt into rock faces. The fishing is tentative until Tom adopts an old Montana standby—a Bitch Creek nymph as dropper with a Wooly Bugger on the point, dead-drifted with lots of scope into the deep pools—and it is the right rig at the right time. From then on we catch fish steadily for the rest of the day, most of them the pale, hard-fighting Kamloops strain we met yesterday in the Missouri.

At the take-out, after nearly twelve hours on the river, Graham says it is the best day he has ever had on the Dearborn.

We are joined for dinner at the Dearborn Inn by one of Graham's guides, a thin, bearded carpenter named Dave Ames, who tells, between soup and dessert, two affecting, detail-rich road stories about loss. One story features a client who up and died on him of an aneurysm while hiking out of a canyon after fishing. Looking perfectly normal, the client sat down beside a tree, said, "Oh boy," and died with his eyes open. The other story is about a tarpon Dave fought for three hours from the shore on the island of Anegada, from the end of a late-night party into dawn, and finally lost to a shark. Dave described seeing the two halves of his fish, the front half still trying to swim, drifting out on the tide. For some reason, I ask him if he is married. He is palpably a private man, and I am immediately sorry I asked this question.

"I had a very unhappy wife," he says after a moment, and smiles.

Later Dave tells me that if we are going to call this a real Montana road trip, we have to shoot up at least a couple of road signs. He also tells us about the Battle Creek Ranch lakes outside of Choteau, and we decide to try them out the next day on our drift north.

◆　　◆　　◆

Choteau was a town I liked. Surrounded by rich ranch land but with the Front Range of the Rockies right there to remind people every time they look west that they are nothing more than human, it seemed a prosperous but modest, friendly place. There was the Munch and Lunch Restaurant, and the Foothills Woman Gift Shop, and men ambling around in big hats, with snuff cans making circles in the back pockets of their jeans. A Triangle Meat Company truck announced with Western forthrightness that that company was "Hog enough to want your business, man enough to appreciate it."

A man named Perry, who ran a tire store in town, directed us to the lakes. The country's biggest dinosaur dig was on the road out to Battle Creek, he told us. The dig was mostly staffed by city folks, easterners, he said. "They pretty much treat us like a bunch of low-life, brain-dead, small-town motherfuckers. Those guys would really like you all," he said, seeming to mean it as a compliment. "They're used to the new."

One answer to the attrition of available trophy-trout water around you is to create your own, which is what Jack Salmond has done on his forty-thousand-acre Battle Creek Ranch. Located thirty miles of dirt road from Choteau, right up against the Front Range at the edge of the Lewis and Clark National Forest, in the middle of hundreds of square miles of grasslands and nothing else, the ranch has been in Salmond's family since the first whites settled this area of Montana late in the last century. It was once owned by his grandmother, Elizabeth Collins, the Cattle Queen of Montana, whose life became the subject of a movie by that title starring Barbara Stanwyck and Ronald Reagan. Some years ago Salmond began experimenting with raising trout in a number of fifteen-to-twenty-acre man-made lakes on the ranch, and found the growth rates of the fish so satisfactory that he decided to open the lakes to fee fishing. Now he has an attractive, modern lodge that sleeps eight, and seven lakes holding brookies, browns, and Kamloops rainbows, which, in two of the lakes, average an honest five pounds and run as heavy as eight to twelve.

There are more and more of these carefully and expensively managed fly-fishing kiosks on private lakes throughout the West, and there will certainly be more yet. Salmond's is one of the best, and if you want to catch trophy trout and have more money than time to do it with, Battle Creek Lodge is a fine place to find yourself almost anytime during the June-through-September season.

Salmond was away in Oregon, so we fished two of the lakes with Justin Hilgendorff, his head guide. Wading out of the first one at 6:30 P.M., we found our neoprenes covered with the maggoty, gray-green waterbugs called scuds. Justin pointed out that the amazing stew of scuds, shrimp, damselflies, dragonflies, midges, caddises, and snails in the lakes is what accounts for the phenomenal trout growth rate of a pound to a pound and a half and six to seven inches a year. Figuring from that information that scuds had to be powerful good for you, Tom and I scooped a few off our waders and tried them. They had the dull tastiness of snails, but moved around more as you ate them.

Young Justin watched us with a good Western effort at disguising his horror. "I don't reckon we'll forget you fellas," he said.

Tired and hungry for something more than scuds, and not being much of a lake-fishing enthusiast anyway, I drove back to Choteau around eight o'clock. Tom and Tim fished with Justin until dark. Between them, on a late hatch of caddis, they caught around a dozen fish, and the smallest of those was over three pounds.

Yesterday we drove through the Blackfoot Indian town of Browning, then up into the conifers and ragged stone spires along the southern boundary of Glacier National Park to West Glacier, where we had the best and biggest burger of the trip at the Conoco station restaurant and talked to the young partners at Glacier Wilderness Guides about fishing the Middle Fork of the Flathead River for the big west-slope cutthroats we had heard were running there. But the float didn't make a strong enough case for itself, so we drove on, into windy, showery northern weather, through Kalispell, then west on Highway 2.

"While making a living, make room for life," a sign in Kalispell told us, and we did just that a few hours later on the ravishingly pretty little Thompson River. Once you pass McGregor Lake and enter the Kootenai National Forest on Highway 2, you seem instantly to leave Montana and enter the tall evergreens and ragged, untended-looking country of the Pacific Northwest. The Thompson ran caramel-colored and four to eight feet across through big stands of Ponderosa pine, Douglas fir, Engleman spruce, larch, and hemlock. Tom and Tim fished downstream of the public campground where we parked, and I fished upstream with a dry fly over a nymph on a 2-weight rod, and made room for life by plucking a dozen or so spunky six-to-ten-inch rainbows out of jaunty little runs that reminded me of New Hampshire brook trout water.

We fished the Thompson from five to seven, then drove on into Libby, showered and dropped our gear at a motel, and headed out to the Red Dog Saloon to meet up with Chris Child and Dan O'Brien, who had driven up from Utah and South Dakota to join us for the last sitting of the feast.

A road-angling trip should always include some *terra incognita*. For Tom and me, this Kootenai country that Tim has been so impatient to show us is it, and we have saved it for last.

◆   ◆   ◆

In 1986, Tim Linehan moved from New Hampshire to the Yaak Valley of Montana, wanting to be a hunting and fishing guide in remote, beautiful country, and now he is that—taking people fishing on the Kootenai River and a few of its tributaries, hunting for elk and deer in the mountains, and shooting in the evergreens for ruffed grouse over his golden retriever. He and his bright and pretty wife and partner, Joanne, live in a wood-heated cabin in Yaak, a town with two bars and one general store, an hour-and-a-half drive north of Libby. It is shaggy, green, mountain-man country, with an aura to it as strong as train smoke. Its inhabitants are few, scattered, and independent, and they tend to have a passionate and protective love for the valley.

Part of what Tim loves about his neck of the woods is its fishing—which is rebounding quickly from considerable degradation caused by excessive logging during the Reagan and

Bush administrations, but is still virtually unknown compared to the glamourpuss rivers of southwestern Montana—and he is anxious to introduce us to it and a little nervous about how it will show itself.

The major river of the fishery is the Kootenai, and we float a six-mile stretch of it in the afternoon after sleeping off a late night of pizza and steak and many pitchers of beer with Chris and Dan at the Red Dog. Dan O'Brien is a writer, a falconer, and a trainer of English setters. Chris Child sells real estate in Park City and was, for a while, my good-hearted partner in a sporting travel company. The three of us follow a bird-hunting movable feast each fall in Canada, and I know Chris and Dan to be nomadic revelers of the highest order.

We go up to Mel Siefke's house to rent a raft for these boys of mine. Mel is a taxidermist. He has lion dogs chained up outside, deer heads and mountain lions on his wall, and a six-pound brook trout in his freezer that someone has brought for him to mount. Where might this substantial brook trout have been angled? we wonder. Locally, Mel says; he can put us in touch with a guy who knows. And suddenly another valley appears and shimmers before the wearying road-anglers.

The Kootenai below Libby Dam is a wide, big-shouldered tailwater that is Montana's second largest river by volume. Its water is a glacial slate blue, running in a thick, even, deceptively slick-surfaced surge, and pooling into great, lightless holes that look like big-fish condos and are: the state record rainbow of twenty-nine pounds came out of one of them. We have a breezy, cool, tall-cloud afternoon under the steep, furrowed gaze of the Cabinet Mountains to the south, and fish mostly small dries to pods of rising fish in the current seams behind islands and in slicks along the banks. The rainbows we catch are plump and acrobatic and as chalky as the water.

After another good late supper at the Red Dog, we drive over the hill to the Yaak Valley and go to sleep in the Overdale Lodge. I don't see much of the place. I walk upstairs, drop my duffel in one of the bedrooms, and don't even remember turning out the light.

It is like waking up in the Peaceable Kingdom. From the large, cheerful, food-stocked kitchen where I make coffee, I look out on trout ponds, Canada geese and goslings, a hardworking osprey, and embracing, thickly evergreened hills. At Overdale there are trout to catch in the ponds, horses to ride, trails to hike, and ranch dogs to follow you around as you stroll the meadows, gathering your piscatorial energy for another day, your twelfth, on the water.

Today that water is a charming little tributary of the Kootenai, the name of which Tim doesn't want bandied about, and I don't blame him. Call it Tiffany. Yaak Valley writer Rick Bass meets us in midafternoon and the six of us float eight miles of this sweetheart in two boats and a raft until dark. It is a cool, damp day with periods of rain and some spectacular plays of light during breaks in the clouds. Tiffany has dark water and meanders brightly during the first few miles into riffles and pools, then straightens and strolls, her banks in this lower section buxom with willows. There are lots of ducks, Canada geese, unshy deer. There is a small hatch of bluewing olives out for much of the afternoon, and six-to-fourteen-inch brookies and rainbows take parachute Adamses and elkhair caddises happily and scream around in the cold, tea-colored water. We have to drag the boats over a tree after it resists Rick's and Tim's efforts to cut it in half with a chainsaw that Rick has brought along with him like a lunch. Chris and Dan take turns rowing their raft and fish hard, gnawing away on the day like a haunch of beef. Tom and I can hear them making merry from a half-mile away all afternoon. In the last row-out mile or two of slow water, in the near-dark context of God knows what kind of conversation, Chris asks Dan what he would reply to King Arthur, should that personage appear on the banks astride his horse and offer to throw them a line for a tow. "We'll take 'er, Art," says Dan. "Want some chaw?"

Joanne cooks dinner for all of us at the lodge tonight: elk steaks, chicken breasts, and bear sausage, squash stuffed with rice and lentils, fresh green beans and a salad, good wines and a fudge pie. It is the finest feasting yet, on this penultimate night of the trip.

❖   ❖   ❖

June 17. Mel Siefke has given us the name of the man in the know on the six-pound brook trout, and Tim has called him up. For our last afternoon of fishing he has agreed to take us into a series of beaver ponds near Libby where that fish and some others like it came from. Greg is the man's name. He tells Tim on the phone that he and his group did not catch all of the big ones out of the ponds, and the ones they didn't catch should still be there, including one of over twenty inches.

We follow Greg and a friend of his named Glen down a long, potholed dirt road to four small beaver ponds lying in an enormous meadow that holds the remains of a homesteader's cabin and graveyard and is snugged up to the very base of the Cabinet Mountains, one of the last remaining grizzly bear strongholds in the lower forty-eight. It is coming on six o'clock. The late light of this clearing afternoon has turned the meadow a Van Gogh gold. Waifish little wisps of cloud glide in and cling to the mountain's skirts. It is as beautiful a last valley for this trip as any you could imagine, and I wader up as hurried along by imagination as I was on the Ruby almost two weeks ago. It is impossible to know, after all, from valleys before what holds in any new water: a brook trout as big as the Ritz? Old Mossyback? Some Last Word in fish?

Chris and Dan go off in one direction, and Glen, Tim, and Tom in another. Greg graciously leads me over to the pond where he and his friends had left one hog uncaught a few weeks ago. We study the shallow, peaty water from a distance. We whisper about the exact whereabouts of the fish's lie and what he might enjoy for a snack. Then I tie on a fly, walk as close as I dare, crouch, and make this final new water come real with a cast—the fly line unrolling along a plane between future and present, then dropping onto the pond's still surface a question demanding an answer.

After five or six more casts, Greg says, "He's gone. We'd have seen him move to the fly or spook if he was still in there." I already know that this is our bleak answer here—having just spotted near my feet a recently discarded cardboard worm container. Greg and I go try another of the beaver ponds. There are fresh tire tracks leading into this one, another worm container on the shore.

We walk back to the vehicles and meet the others. No one has seen a fish except Glen, who casts for a while to one shell-shocked brookie hiding under a log, perhaps the last fish in these ponds.

Cigars are lit and a long-necked bottle of Dickel is passed around as we break down the rods to laughter and another gathering dark. When the bottle comes around to me, I take a pull to that Old Mossyback no longer here, somebody's supper or mount, the payoff to someone's trip down a potholed road, then take one more to whoever caught him. A kid maybe, I think: a road-angler in training.

C O L L I S I O N   A T

H O M O S A S S A

EACH SPRING THEY SLIDE INTO THIS PLACE, COMING FROM the deep waters of the Gulf of Mexico. One day this stretch of shallow water on either side of the river's mouth will be practically lifeless—a few scuttling rays, a prowling tiger shark, a school or two of bait fish—and the next, as if someone had waved a wand, there will be tarpon everywhere, thousands of them, bright as a brass band, bringing the water alive with their silver gathering. They come from the south—that is all anyone knows—and when they leave in little more than a month, they will go north. People will spot a few of them off Apalachicola, Florida, and Pass Christian, Mississippi, and the Chandeleur Islands of Louisiana, and Port Aransas, Texas, as they make their way westward toward Mexico, but they won't be seen again anywhere else in the world in the numbers they are seen here at the mouth of the Homosassa River on the west coast of Florida between the middle of May and the middle of June.

Most saltwater gamefish live like Greek playboys, following pleasure and abundance from one sunny spot where the living is good to the next. Though no one is sure of this, the tarpon probably come to this particular place for the pleasures and abundance of sex. One may imagine them coming in from the deep water at night, on a rising tide, under a waxing three-quarter moon, sensing the landmarks, the certain and particular characteristics of the place, and then registering pleasure or relief from the instincts switching off that brought them to it—like getting off a train late at night, and recognizing, just from the way the air feels, a place you are happy to have traveled a long way to return to; and like, then, taking a deep breath and feeling yourself relax.

It is not a large place—two or three miles wide from the mangrove islands to deeper water, and maybe ten or twelve miles long from Pine Island, south of the river's mouth, to the St. Martins Islands north of it. Throughout, the water has an average depth of about eight feet and a temperature, when the place is perfect, of around eighty degrees Fahrenheit. It is salt water freshened by the flow of 600 million gallons a day from the Homosassa River, and it is very clear. Near the southern end, around the area known as "Oklahoma," the bottom is white; at Black Rock and around the bird racks and off the point, the white sand is mottled by a green-brown sway of turtle, moss, and needle grasses. There are a few deep channels, but mostly the place is one big flat, eight feet or so of clear water over a variegated bottom, and unexceptional except for whatever about it causes these returning herds of tarpon to take a deep collective breath and stay to dally.

◆　　　◆　　　◆

At eighty pounds, this particular tarpon is a little smaller than the average here and a good bit smaller than the largest, making him, more than likely, a male. It is his second year returning to the place. He came into it last night in a school of a hundred fish, joining hundreds of others already arrived. Physically, like those others, he fits this earliest scientific description of his species, published in a Latin book in Amsterdam in 1658:

Among common sea fish is found the Camaripunguacus,
*which at maturity attains the bulk and size of a man and
is exceedingly fat. It possesses a very large toothless mouth,
its lower jaw fixed and its upper shorter. The eyes are large
and silvery; its tail broad, somewhat forked; and to its dorsal fin when erect there is a long appendage attached like a
thick rope running straight toward the tail. The entire
fish is covered with scales which are closely placed upon it,
and so beautifully diversified is the silver with the blue
that it seems coated as if with pure silver.*

When the sun rises, the silvery, eighty-pound male tarpon is
crisscrossing the flat in patterns that the place itself designs,
swimming unhurriedly just below the surface, the opaque tip of
his dorsal fin and the top fork of his tail occasionally breaking
the surface, near the middle of a shifting, regimental line of tarpon three or four fish wide and over fifty fish long. Because he
is a young tarpon, he will travel with this school all day, following its pattern over the flat, learning the place, feeding rarely
and without much interest, and breaking from time to time
with other fish from the school into the circles known as "daisy
chains." It may be that daisy chains are what these fish are here
for. One of the sea's solemn, ceremonial mysteries, they are
probably spawning circles, in which a number of male tarpon
swim nose-to-tail around one big female or more; when the
female drops her eggs, the smaller males rush in from the edges
of the circle, whirling their silver sides up, competing to spray
the eggs with sperm. Between the flash and spending energy of
the chains, the eighty-pound male tarpon moves with the
school in easy sweeps over the flat, unrushed for the time being
by the urge to breed or feed, and unbothered in this place
where big sharks are rare by fear of his one natural enemy, with

whom he has shared shallow water since the Mesozoic. Of his other enemy here, unnatural, above the surface, he is unaware until later that morning.

There is slick calm at eleven o'clock. The water is a glassine envelope, and above it, through its unruffled silver break with the air, the tarpon's round eye might make out a stick-figure rhythmically waving a high wand against a pale blue sky. The fish is along one edge of the school, swimming eastward. Two feet in front of him, something appears, moving through the water in slow, short surges. Four inches of chicken feathers wrapped to a hook, it looks to the tarpon like a thing very easy to eat; perhaps it makes him mad. Without changing course or speed, he opens his mouth and sucks the thing in. There is a slight tug at the corner of his mouth, and then a sudden jerk. The tarpon snaps his head away from the jerk and thrashes, and the school bolts away to the north. There are five more quick jerks at the corner of the tarpon's mouth, and then a steady pressure there as the fish runs after the school; a hundred yards out, he jumps, twisting three feet out of the water and rattling his head to shake the pressure. For the next half hour the fish runs and jumps and tosses his head against that pressure, and with every movement lactic acid builds in his muscles, finally closing him down, reducing his struggle to weak circles against the pull drawing him upward toward a long black shadow on the surface. When he is there, a silver hook slices through the water, trailing bubbles, pinning his lower lip to the shadow. There is movement like a crawl of worms inside his mouth, and then, as inexplicably as being suddenly caught, he is suddenly free, drifting away from the shadow, his gills flaring for oxygen, his flesh knotted with exhaustion.

◆　　　◆　　　◆

The shadow is the hull of a boat. The boat is called the *Tarpon Fly*. Inside it, Billy Pate watches the tarpon swim slowly away, then he checks his fly and leader for any damage the fish might have done to them. The *Tarpon Fly* is one of twenty-two similar boats—sixteen-to-twenty-foot skiffs with big engines and clear decks—that are out on this flat today, all within sight of each other, all fishing for tarpon. In practically every boat there are only two people: one, a professional guide, stands on a platform over the engine in the stern, poling the skiff; the other, an angler, stands in the bow, usually on another platform, holding a rigged fly rod, an assemblage of tackle not much larger than the fly outfits used in fresh water to catch three-pound bass. They are here off the mouth of the Homosassa River to stalk and catch big tarpon on this very light tackle, and they are, almost all of them, among the world's most expert and dedicated at doing that. More than the numbers, it is the size of the tarpon here that draws them to this place for this month every year. Nowhere in the known fishing world are more big tarpon found in clear, shallow water than here. Numerous 200-pound fish are seen and hooked here every spring, though one of these has yet to be caught on fly tackle, and that catching remains the unbroken four-minute mile of tarpon fishing, the big dream that pulls most of these anglers back year after year. And for the past two years the world fly-rod record for tarpon has been set here, two years ago by Billy Pate with a 182-pound fish, and last year by Tom Evans, who upped the record to 186½.

Though many tarpon are caught at Homosassa, very few are killed. Since they are all but worthless as a food fish, and since the great majority of the anglers here have no interest in hanging one on a wall, the only tarpon brought into the dock as a rule are ones believed to be potential records. The small male tarpon Billy Pate has just released was neither 200 pounds nor a new world record, neither of the things Pate is here for, and so he was freed. Very likely, tarpon do not care how much they weigh—but for this one, caught and released by perhaps the finest fishing athlete in the world, a 106 pounds or so was a matter of life and death.

◆　　　◆　　　◆

Like other world-class athletes, Billy Pate works more than plays at what he does. He holds and has held more significant saltwater fly-rod records than any angler ever, and though many of those records are for billfish (he was the first angler to catch all six of the major billfish on a fly), tarpon are the heart of his work. Since 1964 he has spent more than a hundred days a year fishing for them in southern Florida and the Keys, in the Yucatán, Honduras, Costa Rica, Africa, Nicaragua, Brazil, Jamaica, Trinidad, the Bahamas, and Venezuela; and he reckons that in that period, in those places, he has "jumped," or hooked, over two thousand of them.

For the last eight years he has come to Homosassa every May, bringing up his own boat and often his own guide from the Keys where he lives, to fish for thirty days. If that fishing is good (last year he jumped some two hundred fish), it is anything but easy. Generally, Pate spends twelve hours a day on the water, more than eleven of them on his feet, looking for fish, casting precisely to them when he finds them, with tackle that includes, as its weakest link, a single strand of sixteen-pound-test monofilament line. A few years ago on such tackle he fought one tarpon for twelve and a half hours from seven-thirty in the morning until eight at night, without sitting down or eating, until the boat ran out of gas and he lost the fish. When he is not on the water at Homosassa, he is back at the house he rents on the river, studying tide charts, tying leaders, working on his tackle. He is rarely up beyond ten o'clock at night. He eats very carefully and takes over fifty vitamin pills a day, and at fifty-one he is still in perfect shape. Fishing on his level, like the upper reaches of any sport, is a matter of constant training, skill, and the putting together of dozens of little things properly. In this May of 1982, Billy Pate is in Homosassa to reclaim his world record, to catch a tarpon of more than 186½ pounds on a fly rod. He is serious about doing that, and he is leaving absolutely nothing to chance.

◆　　　◆　　　◆

If you have done any fishing at all, it is almost impossible not to wonder what the fish go through in fighting a man, particularly a man as quick and deadly at beating them as Billy Pate. In height (six foot two inches), girth at the widest point (forty-six inches), and weight (192 pounds), I am very close to the size of the tarpon Pate was looking for in Homosassa; so to learn something of what such a fish might endure at his hands, I hooked his fly into my scuba regulator and fought him underwater as hard as I could for as long as I could.

He could have either released or killed me at the end of eleven minutes. But of course I am not a tarpon.

Of the roughly thirty thousand species of fish that inhabit the earth, the tarpon is arguably, pound for pound, the gamest. If gameness is the measurement we use to grade the style and endurance that an animal brings to the act of trying to save its own life, then few animals score as high as the tarpon. Their runs will eat three hundred yards of line before you can pull out and light a cigarette; their twisting, head-rattling jumps sometimes carry them twelve or even fifteen feet above the water, and occasionally into boats where they have killed or maimed fishermen. Big tarpon can kill you with a heart attack, too, by thrilling or tiring you into one, and they never, ever, lay over and quit.

In Homosassa, photographer Armando Jenik and I, in scuba gear, swam with the eighty-pound fish that Pate released for twenty minutes of the thirty minutes he fought it. Tarpon are school fish, and perhaps for that reason this one didn't seem to mind our being there alongside it during its struggle: in full fight it even allowed me to rub my hands down its hard, trout-slick, silver-green sides. There in the water with a hooked tarpon you see how the fish uses its caudal fin in perfect concert with its broad, blunt tail to jump; you feel the sprung energy of its burrowing runs, and its silver quickness, and the fury with which it constantly shakes its head against the intrusion of the hook. And there is no way in this world you cannot admire the tarpon's strength, speed, and endurance, or be moved and more than a little awed by the all-out prodigality of its effort and its absolute refusal to quit fighting until is is either gaffed or released.

But for all his gameness, that fish, at under a hundred pounds, was no match for Billy Pate at Pate's own game, a game he owns.

The next fish he hooked, on the following day, was. The instant Pate saw the big female tarpon turn out of a daisy chain and take his fly, he knew it could be the one he was here for—his record returning to him, or even the two-hundred-pound dream fish, the one he had fished for almost three hundred days over eight years at this place to catch. Hooked, the tarpon made a long, dignified run west, after its school, without jumping once. As his guide, Rick Doyle, prepared to follow, Pate held his rod high, his face thoughtful, watching the line disappear off his reel in the direction of Mexico. His friend Patty

Blair helped him into his fighting belt and glove, and then he and the fish settled in seriously to fight.

Despite all of Pate's skill and readiness, the odds were in the tarpon's favor. What makes sportfishing a sport is allowing the fish an edge. The bigger that edge, within reasonable limits, and the more interestingly the contest is contrived to favor the creature that didn't ask for it, the more challenging the fishing. Extreme sportfishing is a fascination with what is so challenging as to be nearly impossible, such as boating a tarpon of nearly two hundred pounds on a fly rod with a sixteen-pound-test leader. At least nine out of ten such fish, hooked on such tackle, are lost, in any of a dozen possible ways. But this one was not. The hook was well seated in its bony mouth; the leader did not fray; all of Pate's ornate, carefully tied knots held; the drag on his reel didn't slip or freeze; another tarpon didn't swim across the line or a rock cut it. And after three and a half hours Rick Doyle—using a special pair of nonslip gloves, his feet hooked under a special toe-rail built into Pate's boat—crashed a special spaceship-metal gaff into the back of the giant female tarpon, miraculously kept himself from being pulled overboard, and pinned the fish to the boat. All the little things had come together perfectly, and Billy Pate had what he had come here for—the new world record.

Reduced to strung-up meat on the dock, that record weighed 188 pounds. Looking at it hanging next to Billy while various photographers took pictures, and seeing the two of them framed like that—like a photograph of an accident, an odd collision between instinct and ambition—made me hope that fifteen- or sixteen-year-old fish, which, very likely, had been coming to Homosassa for its own good reasons for more years even than Pate, caught out of a daisy chain, had finished what it came there for, too.

THE BIG GAME

RENDERED INATTENTIVE BY VODKA AND VALIUM, A LEG-endary big-game fishing captain was roped to his bunk one evening by playful cohorts aboard a mothership called the *Petaj*, anchored along Australia's Great Barrier Reef. The cohorts completely immobilized the captain except for his right foot, the big toe of which was connected by a string to the ship's bell, so that when he woke and began to struggle, he would find himself paralyzed to the clanging of the "red meanies."

Later this captain took revenge on one of the men who had Gullivered him, another legendary big-game fishing skipper with the nickname of Brazaka, a bearded rouser whose client in those days for much of the black marlin season was the actor Lee Marvin. The offended captain commandeered a helicopter on a hot, calm day, loaded it with dozens of eggs and gallon jugs of ketchup, and flew up the reef, looking for Brazaka's boat. When he found it, he proceeded to bomb it from the hovering chopper. With ketchup and yolk running down his hatches, Brazaka abandoned the tower for the cabin and shouted for his client to join him there. But Lee Marvin, emboldened perhaps by liquid refreshment, stayed on the tower, taking grave hits and waving his fists at the chopper.

"I can't come down, goddammit," he bellowed to Brazaka. "I'm the *hero!*"

◆　　　◆　　　◆

In search of giant black marlin, I lived aboard the *Petaj* myself for ten of the Good Old Days of the 1970s and 1980s, and while I cannot personally guarantee the veracity of the story above, I can say it neatly fits the tenor of that time. And quite a time it was. Hunting marlin by day on a gameboat called the *Hooker*, rock music on the tape player, rum and Coke in hand, a bit of white powder energy enhancer in the galley should it be needed, a couple of eponymous young women from Cairns aboard for making sandwiches, etc. Then around dark you would run in from fishing to the mothership, anchored somewhere along the reef, for an evening of conviviality (drinking games, perhaps more sandwich-making by the young women . . .) and refined competition (the nightly "*Petaj* Olympics" consisted of arm-wrestling, holding a chair upright by one of its legs until it dropped, and racing upside down like howler monkeys along the ceiling framework of the boat's main cabin).

It was a hearty and durable group of immoderates living this fish-till-you-puke life on the *Petaj*: boat manufacturer and international angling's *enfant terrible* Tim Choate; Ronny Hamlin, the infamous "Captain Hook," about whom swirled stories of legendary naughtiness; brash Peter Wright, nicknamed the Lauderdale Mouth, who was fast becoming one of the best big-game fishing captains of all times; and Jody Bright, then one of Wright's deckies, a young, wisecracking, indefatigably cheerful Texan.

I was there as part of a television film crew making a segment for *The American Sportsman*. My first morning on Peter Wright's boat, I took a seat in the fighting chair and popped a Foster's. Bright leaned against the transom, watching the camera and sound men ferry their gear on board from the *Petaj* for the day's shoot.

"So what do *you* do in this ratfuck?" he asked me.

"I'm part of the talent. I get to fish."

"Uh-huh. How do you get to be that?"

"Be a rock star or a movie actor or politician or something."

"So what are you?"

"None of those things."

"So you'd be sort of talentless talent, huh?" said Bright.

"You could say that."

Another pause. "How do I apply for that job?" he asked.

These were lads with tattoos of billfish on their souls—Peck's Bad Boys of angling who neglected to waste time on anything much but fishing and partying or to discriminate between the two, having a nonstop wet dream of fun in a far-away place catching huge fish to loud music with a buzz on. I felt I was among friends.

I also loved the fishing. I had done some blue-water fishing from the time I was ten years old, but on that first trip to Australia I was really a light-tackle angler—a fly-rodder mostly, of high values and refined sensibilities—with no idea of all the fun I had been missing. I had no idea of how a thousand-pound black marlin, rising as suddenly and menacingly as a revolution behind a teaser twenty feet off the stern (with its stubby, wicked, baseball-bat-thick bill slashing the air, its great brown and indigo shoulders pushing a wake, its infinitely wild and unconcerned eye as wide as a butter plate), can cause a grown man to drop whatever he is holding, experience incontinence, even cry out aloud for his mama. I didn't know about how a marlin chasing a bait will "light up" and glow in furious neon throbs, or about the miracle of seeing a half-ton fish clear the water and seem to be push-pinned onto the air like Michael

Jordan, and then the soul-stirring crash of water when it lands. I didn't know about the thrilling physicality of putting the beef of your legs and back and arms into a fleeing weight four or fives times your own; or about the precision and delicacy of touch—a talent rather than an expertise—required to fight big fish well; or about the seamless synergy of effort between an angler, a captain, and a wireman who are all good and have fished together often; or even about how absorbed you can become during the waits between bites in watching the baits, the birds, the wind-lines on the sea, with the torporous but dedicated attention of a polar bear waiting by a seal hole, knowing any second all hell can break loose.

I fell in love with all that on my first big-game fishing trip to Australia, and also with the nomadic nature of the sport: the footloose adventurousness of following fish and seasons across the blue surfaces of the last true wilderness left on earth in quest of the 1,561-pound black, the double-grander blue, hearing every Jimmy Buffett song a thousand times, redemption . . . There didn't seem to be any consensus on the exact whereabouts of the destination, only on the unquestionable importance of the journey. And again, I felt I was among friends.

I remained among them for the next dozen years or so (as I do today, though less strenuously), and during that time I went in search of big-game fish along the Gulf and Atlantic coasts of the United States; in Mexico, Hawaii, Canada, and the Caribbean; in South and Central America, New Zealand, East Africa, Australia again twice; and the islands of the South Pacific. I don't list all this sporting restlessness in order to boast. No doubt I could have built a more productive, wiser life by staying home, sticking to any number of knittings and fishing bass ponds on the weekends. But big-game fishermen do not often lean toward moderation. Once hooked, it can come to seem that everything else can be put off. On hundreds of nights I have gone to sleep in faraway ports, still watching silvery bait trails on the walls of my closed eyes, having forgotten to call home. Blue-water anglers have always stared at the sea more than they need to—maybe because in its unexamined vastness and wildness it seems singularly capable of delivering something at any moment that there are no words amazed enough for: to bust a move that no one has ever seen before.

Pearl (Zane) Grey went to the South Pacific's Tuamotu Islands in 1927 because of reports he had heard in Tahiti of huge yellowish marlin that lived in the waters there, marlin so ferocious that they attacked native canoes with bills protruding from their *lower* rather than their upper jaws. He never found such a fish (neither has anyone else), but it was a quest worth angling for. Grey was the most renowned big-game fisherman of his generation. And with the books and stories he wrote about his fishing adventures around the world, he did more to popularize and romanticize the sport than anyone of any generation, including his near contemporary and fellow novelist Ernest Hemingway.

While Grey was not the writer Hemingway was, Hemingway was not nearly the angler-adventurer that Grey was. There was absolutely no posturing in Grey's motives for fishing and adventuring—he did both as simply and intently as a farmboy putting a cane pole over his shoulder, hiking off to every pond within walking distance, and fishing in them until dark, day after day, not for some new element of a persona, but for the biggest things that lived in the ponds.

Grey loved fishing for big fish as much as any man who ever lived, and he personified the restless, dreaming spirit that is at the heart of big-game fishing and that gives it more in common with high-altitude mountaineering than with other kinds of fishing. At a time when just getting to those places was a major undertaking, he fished in California and the Keys, Nova Scotia, Mexico, Panama, New Zealand, Australia, and all over French Polynesia. He caught swordfish, giant bluefin tuna, sailfish, blue, black, and striped marlin, mako, and thresher shark—more of the major big-game species by far than any angler of his time. On his third trip to Tahiti he caught a 1,040-pound Pacific blue marlin, the first fish of over a thousand pounds ever taken on rod and reel. No one caught another "grander" for twenty-two years.

◆　　◆　　◆

In 1992, Jody Bright—by then a world-traveling big-game fishing captain—and I and a small group of stalwarts went to the Tuamotus ourselves, also questing. Jody was looking for Big Mama, a Pacific blue marlin larger than the world-record 1,376-pound female caught off of Kona, Hawaii, by skipper Bobby Brown's boat on a day when Jody was supposed to be Brown's wireman but jumped onto another boat to help out a friend. For the past few years Bright had been studying commercial fishing catch reports from Japanese, Korean, Taiwanese, Australian, Indonesian, and U.S. long-liners. Those reports break down the Pacific Ocean into five-degree latitude boxes and report the number of hooks being fished in each box, the number of vessels fishing them, and the monthly catches there by species. By dividing the number of blue marlin caught into the overall monthly weight of the catch, Bright was able to identify the average size of the fish concentrated in particular areas for particular months. Amazingly, no sport fisherman had ever done this before.

What he found was that the largest concentration of big female blue marlin in the Pacific occurred in the Tuamotus during two months of the southern hemisphere spring. Then, poring over nautical charts of the area, he found shallow markings next to deep water, and by drawing a line between those markings, like connecting the dots, he discovered the outline of a bank.

It was the exact place where Big Mama might live, he told me over the phone—maybe part of the undiscovered breeding grounds for the Pacific blue marlin. And where was this unnamed bank, exactly? Somewhere in the Tuamotu Archipelago, was all Jody would say. But that was enough. My own quest was less ambitious than his or Grey's. Though I had paid in thirty-something years of dues to marlin fishing, I had never caught a Pacific blue, or any marlin over five hundred pounds; I wanted nothing more from the Tuamotus than to put those two together.

On the forty-seven-foot Buddy Davis gameboat we had had brought down from the Society Island of Tahaa, we did a few days of warm-up fishing around Rangiroa, the most populated island of the Tuamotus, in water that no more than three or four boats had fished in the sixty-five years since Grey had been there looking for his yellowish marlin with the underslung bill. Jody was the captain; I was the angler; David Beaudet, whom Jody had brought over from Kona, was the wireman.

Though some captains will tell you they can put a marlin in the boat with a corpse in the chair if the corpse can reel, the beauty and thrill of big-game fishing resides in the teamwork between captain, wireman, and angler. The bigger the fish, the more important that teamwork becomes. The angler hooks and fights the fish, adjusting the drag and his own labor to react to whatever the fish is doing, to keep it off balance and turn its head as often as possible. The captain anticipates his angler and uses the boat and the sea conditions to help him. The wireman keeps the angler facing the fish by turning the fighting chair, advises him on drag or reel gearing the way a caddy advises a golfer on clubs, and then wires the fish when it is ready. (This last is one of the diciest duties on earth: in big-game fishing you are allowed up to thirty feet of wire leader, which is connected to your line at one end by a swivel and to your bait or lure at the other end; an angler can fight a fish up to the boat with a rod only so far as the swivel, and it then becomes the wireman's unenviable job to bring the fish the rest of the way in for gaffing or release by wrapping one hand in front of another around a thirty-foot piece of galvanized wire that breaks at about four hundred pounds of pressure, and hauling the fish into the transom.)

When everyone knows his job and this teamwork is smooth, you are big-game fishing; otherwise you're just ripping lips, and putting your health at risk while you're at it. Carelessness and inexperience with either big-game tackle or fish can hand you your ass in an ugly variety of ways. One-hundred-thirty-pound-test line unspooling against forty-plus pounds of drag can lop off fingers, even hands. Gaff points and bills can skewer you. David Beaudet has been gored by a bill in the chest and had his left hand broken by a marlin. Less fortunate wiremen, becoming entangled in the wire or caught on the trailing hook of a lure, have been hauled off boats and drowned. Anglers, too, have been pulled overboard or gored, sometimes fatally. And for a final, vivid illustration of faulty teamwork in the pursuit of large fish, think of Ahab.

At eleven-thirty on our second morning out of Rangiroa, while trolling the corner of a huge school of yellowfin tuna, a big marlin bill sliced up behind the left outrigger lure. The fish swirled at the lure and missed it, then charged the lure on the left flat-line, swirled again, and disappeared.

"Try reeling in fast about twenty yards," said David Beaudet. Leaving the rod in its holder on the arm of the fighting chair, I reeled in twenty yards of line, making the lure skip, then let it troll again, and the fish immediately ate it in a boil of water. I heaved the rod out of its holder, carried it into the chair, fixed the butt into the gimbal, clipped the kidney harness into the reel, and watched the line pour off the big, gold anodized-aluminum reel against forty pounds of resistance.

When the fish's run was over, I leaned into the harness, pumping the rod in short strokes, dropping and reeling, and looking through muscle memory for the exact timing of exerted effort by legs, back, and arms that makes for the right combination of force and smoothness. The fish jumped twice, showing weight carried all the way back to its tail, then settled down and fought deep. We were only about five hundred yards off the reef of Rangiroa, and I could watch palm trees bouncing to the trade winds. Boobies dove into a bait school a hundred yards off the stern. Beaudet swung the chair for me, Jody handled the boat, and I gloried in the paced, sweaty, totally absorbing joy of balancing strength against strength. "I did not think. I only felt," wrote Zane Grey about this joy, which is the red, beating heart of big-game fishing. "How blue the sky, wonderful the water, gorgeous the islands!"

Beaudet wired and released the fish inside of fifty minutes. It was not Big Mama, not even by half, but it was my quest fish and more—somewhere around seven hundred pounds. It was one of the first marlin, and certainly the largest, ever caught in the Tuamotus (Grey hooked but did not catch a marlin there), and along with the five other blue marlin we either caught or lost inside of twelve hours of serious trolling, it proved Captain Bright was on the right track.

Three days later that track finally led us out to his bank in the exact middle of nowhere—the single place in all the Pacific he considered Big Mama most likely to live, a place he had dreamed about fishing and kept to himself for seven years since digging it out of the long-liner reports.

◆　　　◆　　　◆

Sailfish are the most elegant and feminine of big-game fish, and also the showiest on light tackle. They get up to a little over 200 pounds in the Pacific, a little less than 150 in the Atlantic, and should only be fished for with twenty-pound-test line and lighter, or with fly rods. On such tackle, nothing that swims outjumps a hot sailfish. I have seen them greyhound across the water like a skipped stone for over a hundred yards without wetting their backs. And they are wonderful on the bite—rising up out of nowhere like a memory, at first just a brown smudge behind a bait, then a rapier bill cleaving the water, the glorious dorsal fin luffing behind it, then a sudden acceleration, a boil of water . . . Often you will raise two or three, or even four or five, to the baits at the same time, and then to watch the speed (up to seventy miles per hour) and predatory grace of that pack within the pattern, darting between baits, one or two of them lit up and pulsing with blue light, can make you wish for nine eyes.

White marlin, an Atlantic fish, are around the same size as Pacific sails (the world-record white is 181 pounds) and are the most acrobatic and impulsive of the marlin. Like sails, they jump heedlessly on light tackle and they will also fight you deep, but without much conviction. They are jaunty, kickass little fish, and I have had more pure fun catching them than any other marlin.

Striped marlin are a Pacific species, and most of the largest of them (up to nearly 500 pounds) are caught in the waters off the North Island of New Zealand. In 1984 I spent ten days fishing that water for stripies, a couple of those days on board the *Avalon*, the boat Zane Grey had built and fished from in 1926 when he pioneered the Bay of Islands and discovered the incredible striped-marlin fishery there. Though Grey was essentially a big-marlin fisherman, he loved the striped for its combination of heart (for its size, no marlin pulls longer) and show. I have caught little ones in Hawaii that would jump twenty or thirty times, and one in New Zealand of over 250 pounds that fought like a tuna, never showed himself, and came in dead.

Then there are the swordfish and bluefin tuna, each with a small but fervent coterie of devotees, some of whom will fish for nothing else. Bluefins are power lifters who can sprint—in the upper reaches of the weight they reach (the record is 1,496 pounds), they are almost unimaginably strong and fast. I have had one never slow up for eight hundred yards on 130-pound test with the drag cranked down, and finally freeze the reel, leaving everyone on the boat happy he was gone. Tuna do not jump, but bore against you endlessly and punish you like a bad toothache, often for hours. I have never caught a swordfish, but the big ones (world record 1,182 pounds) are said to combine the stamina and strength of tuna with the glitz of marlin, and many experienced anglers regard these mysterious, nocturnal, cold-current lovers as the greatest of all the big-game fish.

The other two contenders for that title are the black and the blue marlin. Blue marlin are found in both the Atlantic and Pacific Oceans, and are the species of choice for more anglers than any other big-game fish. Both blues and blacks (which are found only in the Pacific), can swim at speeds of up to forty-five miles per hour in bursts, and prime animals in the 400-to-600-pound range can maintain runs of over twenty miles per hour for fifteen or twenty minutes, often jumping as they run. Blacks, with their shorter, broader bills and usually greater girths up front for their lengths, are like pro football tackles and guards, while blues are defensive ends. Blacks tend to jump straighter up and down than the greyhounding blues, and to fight deeper. The males of both species rarely get over 300 pounds; the females . . . no one really knows. The largest legally live caught blue, an Atlantic, weighed 1,402 pounds; the largest black, 1,560 pounds, was caught in Peru by Alfred Glassell in *1953*, which illustrates the indomintability of the giant females of that species.

Lots of reliable people swear they have seen or hooked and lost or had eaten by sharks, both blues and blacks of 1,600, 1,800, even 2,000 pounds. Mating for Captain Brian Reeves on the Great Barrier Reef a few years ago with angler Frank Sitterly in the chair, Jody Bright had on the wire *nine times* a black that he knows would have smashed Glassell's record—a fish close to 2,000 pounds that came in straight up and down instead of suspended, so the entire crew couldn't lift it and had to just stand there at the transom and watch a pack of sharks eat it—this marlin that everyone is fishing for—all the way up to the pectoral fins.

The biggest regulation tackle is rendered puny by such fish, and many of them simply cannot be caught on rod and reel except through sublime cooperative skill and freaky good luck. Which is exactly why trying to catch them—the Big Mama blue, the Big Mama black—has been and remains the ultimate quest, the Holy Grail, to many anglers.

◆   ◆   ◆

Zane Grey caught his 1,040-pound Pacific blue marlin in 1930, kicking off the golden decade of big-game fishing. In the following year, Ernest Hemingway bought a house in Key West, and in 1932 he made his first visit to Cuba, there discovering marlin, about which he wrote brilliantly and thoroughly three years later in his chapter called "Marlin Off Cuba" for the book *American Big Game Fishing*.

In 1935 Hemingway took his boat, the *Pilar*, over to the island of Bimini in the Bahamas, where Michael Lerner and others had begun trying to catch giant bluefin tuna, and became the first angler to put one of those sea-oxen into the boat whole, before the sharks got to it. Subsequently, Bimini became the center (along with wherever in the world Zane Grey was) for big-game fishing's heyday. Sports such as Lerner, Tommy Shevlin, Mr. and Mrs. Oliver Grinnell, Kip Farrington, and Philip Wylie (whose "Crunch and Des" books introduced many a young, would-be angler, including myself, to the dream world of big-game fishing), and great, innovating guides such as captains Bill Hatch, Johnny Cass, and the incomparable Tommy Gifford all fished out of Bimini in the thirties.

Some of those anglers were also beginning by then to venture farther abroad, as Grey had been doing for years—to Cape Breton, Central America, Bali, Ecuador, Chile, Peru. A few of them (Lerner and Hemingway, for example) were fine amateur naturalists, and more was learned about big, oceangoing fish and how best to fish for them in a shorter period of time during the thirties than ever before or since. In 1939 Lerner and others formed the International Game Fish Association (IGFA), given over to record keeping, scientific curiosity about gamefish, and the purveying of a "universal code of sporting ethics to guide ocean anglers in their pursuits."

But, as with other golden eras, decay was not far behind the height of bloom. Throughout the thirties, tackle was getting bigger and more brutally efficient. As a result, larger fish were being caught, killed (virtually all of them), and compared competitively. Reputations and careers, along with some fair-sized egos, came to depend on the weight of fish hung up on a dock. By 1940 big-game fishing was already infected with too much testosterone and becoming something other than what it had been. For a sort of stop-action photo of that metamorphosis, we have Marjorie Kinnan Rawlings's description of Hemingway near the end of the decade, roaring drunk and alone late one night on the dock at Bimini, using the hanging carcass of a 514-pound bluefin he had caught that day for a punching bag.

It is more or less a straight line from that Bimini dock to the *Petaj*, anchored along the Great Barrier Reef in the early eighties—where thousand-pound female marlin were hung up on gin poles to be photographed, and then were thrown to the sharks, and any fish under five hundred pounds was referred to as a "rat"; where the price tag for a week's fishing could run as much as $50,000, a case of herpes, and a two-month hangover. For a while, there and in other parts of the world, big-game fishing fully became the Animal House of the blood sports.

But things are different now, even on the Great Barrier Reef. Three or four years ago, when I was back there staying at the splendid Lizard Island Resort, I spent a pleasant afternoon aboard one of Australia's newest luxury motherships, whose crew were proud veterans of many and various immoderations during the Good Old Days. One of the hostesses on board served our group chablis and cheese until she realized that we too had been to the barbecue in the seventies and eighties— then she broke out the tequila and slammer glasses. In between demonstrating her version of the Layback-Slammer—wherein she sat on a stool with her back to the bar, her head and neck extended onto it, while the mothership's chef poured tequila and lime juice into her mouth from separate bottles—and other personal favorites, this hostess commented that her slamming had gone a bit rusty from lack of practice. The new clients were different, she said, momentarily wistful: no drugs, don't drink anything but wine, in touch with their offices every day, never kill a fish. "Some of them even bring their bleeding wives," she sighed.

It is a good thing the new clientele is not inclined to kill fish. Like so much else in the natural world that is unspeakably and irreplaceably valuable, big-game fish stocks have been put gravely at risk in the last few decades of this closing century. A 1996 report from an international group of government officials and biologists suggests that the Atlantic blue marlin population, for example, is just 25 percent of what is necessary to keep pace with increasing fishing pressure. Bluefin tuna have been in serious trouble for years. So have swordfish. Because of commercial overharvesting, even sailfish are endangered in some places, including Costa Rica, which was until just a few years ago arguably the top sportfishing destination in the world for Pacific sails. Planetwide demand for food fish, including all of the big-game species, keeps increasing with exploding populations. In response, government-subsidized fleets have expanded rapidly, and corporate or "factory-style" fishing—abetted by tremendous recent improvements in marine and satellite technology—has created a growing and by now close to uncontrollable drain on the world's big-game fishery resources. Dead-serious and effective organizations such as the Billfish Foundation, IGFA, the National Coalition for Marine Conservation, the Hawaii Conservation Association, and the Coastal Conservation Association are laboring hard to plug that drain, but they need coordinated worldwide cooperation to really make a difference, and that cooperation is hard to come by. Without it, since big-game fish are pelagic and migratory, a blue marlin caught, tagged, and released by some enlightened sport in South Carolina is likely to end up as flash-frozen steaks on a factory boat off Senegal only a few months later.

Maybe there will be billfish and tuna to fish for and be amazed by well into the next century, and maybe not. But in the meantime, there are more lines in the water than ever, and wetting those lines nowadays is a diverse lot of anglers. Most of them are day fishermen, who shell out an average of $650 to $1,000 plus tips and lunch in Cape Hatteras and Cape May, Destin, Nantucket, Port O'Connor, Cabo, and Cozumel to drag baits for eight hours and go home sunburned with or without a fish story. Then there are the tournament anglers. Big-game fishing tournaments have recently become a big industry in the United States, Mexico, and the Caribbean, with pots between $500,000 and $1 million not uncommon, and they have bred a particular kind of fisherman. He owns a Hatteras as big as your front yard, and flies in top captains and wiremen from as far away as Australia to crew the tournaments he goes to in Cozumel in May, North Carolina or Florida or Abaco in July, St. Thomas in August, and Venezuela in October.

Similar to this tournament angler, but also very different, is the world-traveling record stalker. A few of the latter, such as Houstonian Jerry Dunaway, chicken king Don Tyson, and Frenchman Jean-Paul Richard, have (or had, in the case of Dunaway) mothership/gameboat combinations that allow them to follow fish and seasons without the constrictions of land-based accommodations. Dunaway and his wife, Deborah, have between them an astounding fourteen light-tackle billfish world records—including a 102-pound Pacific sailfish on *two-pound-test* line for Mrs. Dunaway—caught from Costa Rica to Dakar. Also from Houston—without a mothership, but with a great gameboat and crew and with three line-class world records on Atlantic blues from the Ivory Coast and Portugal—is Stewart Campbell. Fishing with Peter Wright, Campbell once caught sixty-four bluefin tuna between 300 and 600 pounds in one day, his sixty-fourth birthday—speaking eloquently to the seriousness of intent, as well as to the durability, of anglers of this ilk.

And finally, there are still a few big-game fishermen around who fish primarily and simply to see new water and to find out what's in it: the heirs to Zane Grey.

◆　　　◆　　　◆

I had the privilege of fishing with three of these recently, the same Tim Choate, Ronny Hamlin, and Jody Bright whom I first met on the Great Barrier Reef in 1981. These warhorses of the Good Old Days and I were in Iztapa, on the southwest coast of Guatemala, where Choate owns Fins & Feathers Inn, one of the best saltwater fishing lodges anywhere, on the premier water in the world right now for Pacific sailfish. It is water Choate pioneered, after commercial harvesting began to ruin the sailfishing in Costa Rica, where he had a fleet of boats. Now he is in the forefront of Pacific big-gamefish conservation, working on it with the governments of both Costa Rica and Guatemala. Jody Bright is in that forefront, too. He is founder and president of the Hawaii Conservation Association, and is one of the world's foremost experts on analyzing and patterning the migratory movements of marlin throughout the Pacific, movements that can be used to formulate "best use" recommendations to all the countries sharing the resource.

As for Ronny Hamlin—who was in Iztapa captaining a boat for Choate—he cleaned up well, too. Captain Hook was then fifty-three and reformed from various things, but still inim-

itably blithe, with inimitable *brio*. He began fishing professionally when he was sixteen, and since then has lived and fished
with all four feet in St. Thomas, Cuba, Venezuela, Australia,
and other places, writing and publishing along the way a big-
game fishing novel called *Tournament*. He is a big-marlin spe-
cialist, and has probably seen as many of those formidable
creatures as any man alive. Not far behind him would be
Choate and Bright, and watching the three of them fish for
sailfish, Hamlin driving the boat, while I amused myself inef-
fectually with a fly rod, was a little like watching someone
shoot squirrels with a .30/30.

We drank a lot of Gallo, the excellent Guatemalan beer, and
ate sandwiches of dorado and onions fried together by Hamlin's two well-trained deckies, Haron and José. We told stories
and lies, and laughed more than anything else. There was only
a little rum on board, no white powder in the galley, and the
only sandwich-makers were Haron and José, but the music and
the laughs and the people were pretty much the same as sixteen
years ago. We fooled around with more than thirty sailfish that
came up to bite, taking turns at them. At one point I asked
Captain Hook what he made of all this, having seen more of
everything in the Big Game than almost anyone since 1960.
We were sitting on the flying bridge, and below us on the deck
my wife, Patricia, was catching a sailfish in the fighting chair.
Jody was standing at the transom, dropping back to another sail
and laughing at something Choate was saying, the speed of the
line going off the reel and its angle of entry into the water
telling him things he didn't have to listen to anymore, things it
takes fifteen or twenty years to know that well.

"I'm having fun," said Hamlin, who has always had fun but is
no longer paying too much for it. "You get a little tired of sailfish. But Choate and I are going down to the Cocos Islands in

the summer on a mothership to look around." And then Captain Hook's eyes light up. And so do Tim Choate's later that day, telling me about a pioneer operation he is beginning in Brazil for blue marlin. And so do Jody Bright's eyes light up, talking about trying out new water in the Marquesas, Yemen, the Australs, New Ireland . . . and whenever he talks about returning to his bank in the Tuamotus.

◆   ◆   ◆

Our day there had been a flawless marlin day with a hot, humid, big-fish wind out of the north and just the right chop on the sea. Jody and I watched Nameless Bank come up on the color video depth recorder, right where he knew it would be. Everywhere along it there were birds working and schools of yellowfin tuna crashing bait. David Beaudet dropped the lures overboard, into that water that *no one had ever fished before*, water where a marlin too big even to imagine might live . . . And five minutes later the boat broke. A tiny little thing called an injector seized in the starboard engine of that high-tech, half-million-dollar gameboat, and suddenly we might as well have been out there in the middle of the Pacific in a canoe.

We had to turn around then and head on one engine for the nearest populated island, nursing the boat along for hours at six knots. Jody never looked back at his bank, and "Pioneers get all the arrows" is all he would say on the subject.

Nameless Bank, of course, is still there. And in Captain Bright's mind and mine, at least, so is Big Mama.

THE CLOVE KEY EXPERIMENT

A T ELEVEN O'CLOCK WE STEP OUT OF THE BOAT ONTO A Bahamian bonefish flat of hard, white sand, ideal for wading and for spotting fish. The sun is shining and the wind is light. The tide has just turned and the two feet of water covering the flat is as clear as air.

There are, of course, bonefish everywhere on this flat—did you think there could not be?—and as soon as we spread out and begin walking the flat, the sun and wind both obligingly at our backs, even the tide running with us, we start spotting a school here, a pair of gorillas over there. I cast a perfectly built loop to the second school I see, and naturally the biggest fish in the school grabs the fly and heads for Cuba.

Tom Montgomery, the nonpareil fishing photographer and trout guide, runs over to take another series of lavish cover photos of me grappling with yet another lunker.

Ed and Becky Gray, founders of *Gray's Sporting Journal*, look up from stalking their own fish and watch admiringly as I pass the rod around behind my back from my right hand into my left, then toss it up and catch it by the butt over my head—just a little thing I like to do.

Holding the rod overhead, I sense through its subtle throbbing that this bonefish is bearing down on a coral head a hundred yards away. A flick of the rod tip to the left—the Christmas Island whip, I call it—turns the potential world-record brute in the nick of time, while a second flick to the right bewilders the fish and parks him, as always, in the sand until Tom can get his shot set up.

"What shall we cook for dinner tonight?" I shout gaily to Becky Gray. "Barracuda roe for an appetizer? A little grilled triggerfish with some of that dill pesto in your traveling herb kit?"

"Do you think you can get that bonefish to back up about fifty feet and then sit in the sand again?" Tom asks. "It would improve the angle of the line."

"Ho, ho, ho," I chortle. "Not a problem, Tom." I draw a quick figure-eight in the air with the rod tip and the bonefish shoots backwards for fifty feet and settles obediently to the bottom.

"Nice move!" exclaims Tom, snapping away.

"I call it my Belizean Figure-Eight," I confide, straightening the photogenic bandana at my throat. "That's one you won't see from those stiffs down at the lodge . . ."

Whooaa! I am getting *totally carried away here*—reverting back to those impecunious but thoughtlessly happy days when I made my living writing for hook-and-bullet magazines. Sure, we were all pros out there on that flat—seasoned blood-sport reporters and world-romping gourmands at the top of our games—on the last day of another perfectly planned sojourn to one of those many junctions of Pleasant Street and Easy Avenue that make up the happy map of the outdoors journalist's life. And, well, yes, you might say we were angling trailblazers as well, shunning the lodge on the other end of the island in order to live and fish on our own, without the pesky interference of fishing guides, waiters with little gold rings in their ears, and sunburned, three-jawed chuck manufacturers from Detroit. And you want to know how productive, how effortless, how relentlessly fun our week had been—how we obliged the bonefish on the flats each day by catching them until our arms were sore, then trolled the cuts for giant barracudas and jacks, or perhaps traipsed out to the blue water to wear ourselves thin on wahoo, tuna, and a sailfish or two before going back to our private island for a snorkel, followed by chilled vodka and conch fritters on the deck, another perfect sunset and another perfectly prepared but simple supper . . .

Of *course* you want to hear about all that, and I would love to make it up for you. But unfortunately, I am saddled now with journalistic standards, so all you get from here on in this story is the sordid truth.

◆　　◆　　◆

This particular sojourn started with a letter I received a few winters ago from Becky Gray. As it happened, I was recovering from an operation in the cold and drizzle of Birmingham, Alabama, and I must admit the letter made my heart soar like a virgin's with anticipation of all the sport and creature comfort that Becky described.

> Dear Charles,
>
> We hear you are up and around again, so I am writing to suggest a jaunt, as I am sure you are ready for one. Last year Ed and I took a small group down the Bahamas and rented a wonderful house on its own private island just off the north end of Great Exuma. Can there be words to describe such perfection? The house sleeps and bathes eight, and has its own freshwater source for fairly limitless water. A large deck wraps around the house, so there is always a reason to be outside: breakfast on the deck off the kitchen, rum and tonics on the porch off the living room,

a moonlit gaze at the ocean before bed. The house has a good kitchen and comes with all necessary amenities, including a 25-foot Whaler Outrage boat and a wonderful boatman/caretaker named Tony Smith who will not only drive you to the fishing every day in the Outrage, but will have one of his brothers dive for fresh langouste for your dinner. Tony is a wonder of dependability and organization. He brings over to the house each day crates full of fresh grapefruit, his mother's fresh-baked bread, pigeon peas for famous Bahamian peas and rice, and fresh limes for our rum and tonics. He is also a wonderful chef and will cook dinner whenever we don't feel like doing it ourselves. He keeps the Outrage shipshape and in good running order, and he knows the local water well.

As you know, Ed and I like to find our own fishing, so each day we would pack a lunch and go exploring in the Outrage. So many bonefish flats and so little time! Every day we explored new ones. We'd spend the mornings stalking and casting, watching the birds, eyeing the lemon sharks and rays, and catching bones. Lunch on a white, white sand beach with a swim. Then in the afternoons we would troll between the keys for big barracuda and jacks, etc., or go into the nearby deep water for tuna and bonito, or out to the navy buoy for the big guys.

All this by day. At night (those lovely, balmy nights!) for anyone who hasn't had enough of fishing, you can catch jacks and even big sharks off the dock. The weather is always perfect—day after day of intense, wonderful light that starts in the morning with a warm, still brightness that makes everything, especially the water, sparkle. Mornings melt into hot, tropical afternoons with big, puffy clouds and occasional sprinkles of rain to dust the air with a bit of coolness . . . I'm waxing, I see, but it really is heaven.

In addition to the marvelous fishing and easy living, there is the adventure of exploring all the little deserted islands and finding your own flats. Can you and Patricia join us in March? It's usually the driest month in the Bahamas. We could take along another couple if you like. Say yes.

Much love,
Becky

The trip actually started off perfectly well. We flew into Georgetown, Great Exuma, from Fort Lauderdale on Friday, March 12, to the lovely weather Becky had described in her letter—big, puffy clouds and all that—and lunched at the Peace and Plenty Hotel, where Ed and Becky would be spending a night in order to learn about the hotel's new bonefishing program.

I had fished out of Peace and Plenty with my father back in the sixties, and it is as charming a place now as it was then. Then, you simply hired some local out near the airport with a leaky boat who might or might not know where bonefish were, and if he didn't know, you found them anyway. Now the hotel employs six trained guides equipped with good boats and motors, whose jobs are to know where bonefish are. Given the excellent accommodations and food at Peace and Plenty, its well-equipped guides, and God's own amount of bonefish on countless flats all around Georgetown, it could be wondered why anyone going bonefishing in Exuma would *not* fish out of Peace and Plenty.

One reason might be that do-it-yourself bonefishing, while admittedly a developed taste, has its own strong appeal, and

Exuma is one of the few quality destinations in the world where it can be practiced effectively. To qualify as a do-it-yourself bonefish destination, a place must have plenty of fish on reachable and wadeable flats, some place near those flats where you can camp or stay, and some way to cook or buy your meals. This is a minimum. Personally I would add to that list of requirements a reliable supply of ice cubes and limes, among other things. The Florida Keys; a few other places in the Bahamas; San Pedro on Ambergris Cay in Belize; Cancún, Mexico; and Anegada in the British Virgin Islands are places that fit that bill nicely—but none more nicely than Exuma.

The Grays enjoy all kinds of do-it-yourself fishing, as I do, and we make a habit of prospecting for new opportunities to practice it. The nature of this prospecting is that sometimes you strike it rich, sometimes you don't, but you almost always enjoy the digging.

One of the secrets of getting the best out of any new do-it-yourself location is coming to it well prepared. I had brought along four fly rods of different weights, various fly lines and shooting heads, dozens of bonefish and barracuda flies, a twenty-pound trolling outfit, feather jigs, Konaheads, squid lures, Bonita Expresses, Vortex Chuggers, Front End Cavitators, Side Flow Jets, rigging wire, shark hooks, ballyhoo harnesses, and Tuna Tails. Being geared up for any angling eventuality gives me a feeling of chip-counting smugness. It is probably as close as I will ever come to feeling like a mogul.

Late that afternoon on the ride out to Barre Terre, I went through my tackle as I am wont to do, fondling the lures and flies and sharpening a hook or two. We had left the Grays in Georgetown and were being driven by van to the north end of the island by Tony Smith, caretaker of the house we had rented and our boatman for the week, and his friend Norman. With

Patricia and me was our twenty-six-year-old daughter, Greta, and her friend Scott. Greta has traveled with me before on prospecting fishing trips, most recently to Venezuela in search of baby tarpon. She gave me a bemused, slightly pitying look as I moguled around with my gear.

"Do you think we'll catch anything this time?" she asked.

"Of course. Many huge fish beyond your comprehension. We just had bad tides in Venezuela."

"How about St. Thomas?"

"Wrong phase of the moon. Tony," I said, to change the subject, "we'd like to take out the Outrage tomorrow after bonefishing to catch this child many huge fish in the blue water. How does that sound?"

Tony had seemed a bit distant and preoccupied with his bottle of Kalik beer ever since picking us up at Peace and Plenty. I hoped to draw him into a spirited discussion of our chances with the big pelagics.

"She's broke," he said morosely.

"Who's broke?"

"The Outrage—she's broke," said Tony.

"Sounds like us," Greta sneered.

"*What?* The Outrage is the only boat we have, right? How long she be broke for?" I asked, falling into the ridiculous pidgin dialect I can't seem to help speaking to locals everywhere in the tropics, even ones with Oxonian English.

"We waitin' on a part from the mainland, mon," sighed Tony. "Maybe it come tomorrow. Maybe we cahn fish with my boat." He took a pull on his beer and that was that.

Relax, I told myself: just fall into the easy rhythm of the islands.

The tiny town of Barre Terre was forty-five minutes of rutted road from Georgetown on the northernmost end of Great

Exuma Island. We were to go by boat with Tony from there to our rented house on its private island, called Clove Key. The sun was going down as we reached Barre Terre. Remembering Becky's commendation of Tony's cooking, I hoped he was planning on plying his skill that evening at the house. But when I asked him about supper arrangements, he informed me that he had not had time—what with waiting for the boat part and other pressures—to stock the house with food. We would eat, he announced, here in Barre Terre at the only restaurant in town, one that happened to belong to his friend and our driver out from Georgetown, Norman.

At Norman's Fishermen's Inn, in fact, we drank and dined well on cracked conch, curried mahi-mahi, and green turtle steaks, and when Tony graciously allowed me to pay for his meal and six or seven Kaliks, I sensed he might be finally warming to us.

Clove Key and its house was all Becky had billed it to be. The 160-acre island, Tony told us—perhaps reassuring us over the absence of any food in the house—supported wild goats, chickens, and big land crabs. Sugar cane, kumquats, mangoes, bananas, and coconuts grew on it, and even in the deep dusk of our arrival we could see bougainvillea and hibiscus blazing everywhere. The house had a big vaulted central room, four comfortable bedrooms, and three baths. It was surrounded by a high deck and powered by a generator. A couple from Kansas City had built it in 1972. The man had died recently and the property was now for sale, we learned, which might have accounted for some of Tony's seeming offhandedness. He helped us move our bags from the concrete dock to the house and said he would see us first thing in the morning.

There was a haze glazing the stars, and a breeze rising at a time of day when it should have been falling. I asked Tony what he thought the weather would be like the next day. He appraised the sky and then the sea. "She might blow a little," he said.

I listened to the wind come up all night. By daylight it was blowing a gale out of the south, and the sky was a mass of ominous gray lumps. Tony arrived at seven-thirty with some groceries and other supplies for the house, helped himself to a little rum, and was less than enthusiastic about the day's fishing prospects. We went out anyway, Greta, Scott and I, in Tony's seventeen-foot Whaler. We trolled a couple of cuts between islands without a bite, and then went over to the lee side of a nearby key to look around. There was a big, discolored patch of water there, known as a "mud," that often indicates bonefish feeding on the bottom. I threw a fly into the mud, and a bonefish obligingly slurped it up. I handed the rod over to Greta, who does not fool around with fish. She snubbed up the little guy and hauled him toward the surface. Just as the bonefish showed, we watched a four-foot barracuda eat him. The 'cuda turned toward us, leering and holding the bone crosswise in his mouth. Then he shook his head a couple of times and the leader parted.

"Do you think that's an omen?" said Greta after a moment of silence.

"Of what?" Scott asked her.

"I don't know. That something with big teeth is going to grab our trip and eat it, maybe? Never mind. It's just typical is all."

Scott is a very good trout angler from Wyoming who wanted his first fly-rod fish in salt water to be a bonefish. He and I walked up a little mangrove creek, hoping there would be a fish up there for him. He threw out a few blind casts at the head of the creek, and his first fly-rod fish in salt water turned out to be a six-inch jack. "Let's don't tell Greta," was all he said.

Around ten-thirty the weather went from simply awful to Wagnerian. We ran back to Clove Key in howling wind, stinging rain, thunder and lightning, and *hail*. Hail in the Bahamas! Tony didn't even know what it was.

After a short but miserable boat ride, Tony tied his boat on the lee side of the island and we bushwhacked, shivering in the hail, back to the house over jagged coral, through dripping undergrowth, making our way carefully around gaping sinkholes of black water.

"They're calling it the storm of the century," said Patricia cheerfully. She had been listening to the radio. "Birmingham got *sixteen inches* of snow. Atlanta is totally closed down. New England and New York are buried, and here we are out of it all on our own island in the Bahamas!"

"Have you been outside?" Greta asked her.

We cooked and ate a big, consoling frittata and put some rum in our coffee, then Patricia, Greta, and Scott went back to bed to read, and I went into Georgetown with Tony to talk things over with the Grays and Tom.

I found them in the bar of Peace and Plenty, which was where all the other lodge anglers were. They had gone fishing early and had been driven in by the weather around the same time we were. Becky had asked their guide, a young Bahamian named Steve Ferguson, if bonefish bit well during storms, and Steve had given her this oracular answer: "The bonefish is a peace-lovin' fish, mon. He don' like fuss. He like to be swimmin' along on the bottom just mellowtatin'."

We did a little mellowtating of our own in the bar, and again I bought Tony a number of Kaliks to help soothe his disappointment over the still-missing boat part.

Around six we all headed back to Barre Terre with a friend of mine from Atlanta and his wife, who were staying at Peace and Plenty. It was the friend's fiftieth birthday, a noble occasion, and we had decided to celebrate it at Norman's Fishermen's Inn. We did that, with an enormous meal and many and various libations, and at ten-thirty the Grays, Tom Montgomery, Tony, and I got into Tony's boat to go back to Clove Key. That is normally a fifteen-minute boat ride, but with the roaring wind and steep, high-tide seas slowing us down, it took us thirty minutes of drenching, sobering pitching between the waves just to determine that we would certainly swamp long before we ever made Clove Key. We returned ignominiously to Norman's, and no one there seemed to have noticed we had left. The Grays went off to bed in Norman's spare bedroom. Tom and I took our night's rest in the van, along with a ripening bag of bally-hoo I had bought in Georgetown for bait in the blue water, if and when we managed to fish there.

Steve Ferguson had told the Grays that this was only the second day in five years of fishing that weather had forced him off the water. And it was the first time *ever* that Tony had not been able to make it out to Clove Key. For Tom and me as we stiffened and chilled in the van, one cheering prospect seemed certain—the weather could only improve.

But it didn't. Here, in a mercifully abbreviated version of my journal notes, is an account of the next five days. (For the record, I would love to have thrown a few screaming reels into this account, but journalistic standards would not allow that.)

Sunday, March 14. We leave Barre Terre and make it around the point at six-thirty on a low tide, though the seas and wind are still frighteningly high. Tony's boat running on only two cylinders now, so it takes over an hour to get out to Clove Key, where

Patricia, Greta, and Scott had a sleepless, panicky night, wondering if we had drowned and how they would get off the island if we had. Phone is out at the house, so we couldn't call last night. Phone also out at Norman's, though no one there cares.

Real travelers travel for the journey, not the destination, I remind everyone after we have taken hot showers and had some breakfast, after Tony leaves to go try to get his boat fixed, as we sit staring out at the whipping palm fronds and roiled, unfishable water; and that important bit of philosophy seems to cheer everyone up. Our glass is half full, not half empty, I add. We are not prisoners of this island, but here to enjoy all of its subtle and unexpected pleasures . . . "*Please*, Charles," Becky says then in a small voice, and I realize that my job is done: I have raised all of our spirits as far as they are going to go for the time being.

In the afternoon a thin young man shows up in a turned-around baseball cap and a Bob Marley tank top. This is Bertram, one of Tony's eleven brothers, and he has come in yet another Whaler belonging to another of those brothers. "Tony," says Bertram, "is working on his boat . . . would anyone like to go fishing?"

A few of us troll for a while in the cuts with Bertram, provoking one swirl from a small barracuda.

Delicious grilled chicken and peas and rice for dinner tonight, with a couple of bracing Pinot Grigios. Then Patricia, Becky, and Greta bundle up in all the clothes they can find and go down to the dock to fish for big jacks with conch, one of the many pleasurable options on this do-it-yourself fishing vacation. Ed, Scott, Tom, and I stay behind in the house, hard at another of those options, drinking rum. We enjoy more success with our option than the girls do with theirs: they are back in an hour with wind-chilled faces but no jacks.

Monday, March 15. Still as windy as Tierra del Fuego and cold, the wind having swung now into the northeast. But our hopes are stirred by a few breaks in the clouds. Tony is back, his boat running better, but still no part for the Outrage. We go out to a few little flats to look for bones in the morning. Too windy and cloudy to see, even if there had been anything on the flats other than one lonely leopard ray.

Back at the house for an inspired lunch of deviled eggs and lobster salad that Patricia and Greta put together. The sun comes out for an hour and we all run to the lee deck of the house to sit greedily in it.

In the afternoon, Ed and Becky and I go out with Tony to look for bonefish again. We walk four or five flats without finding a fish, and then come to a final flat, in a lee, just as the late sun slides out from behind the clouds. It is a coral flat, which means the water will be warmer than that on the sand flats, and with sun to see and little wind in the lee, I decide we may have a chance here and determine to bring my thirty years of bonefishing experience and all of my skills to bear at once. I choose a rod with a gray line to minimize the flash from casting; tie up a new sixteen-foot leader tapered to six pounds; choose a secret-weapon fly given to me years ago by a withered old Exuma pro. I put the sun at my back and wade out carefully, my osprey eyes scanning for wakes, or the sparkle of tails, or the chimerical little fish themselves, whose shapes can often seem willed up, formed from under the shimmering skin of water as surprisingly and suddenly as ideas. And then . . . I walk right over the only school of fish any of us have seen in four days—run over them like a cement truck and send forty little unformed ideas scattering. Tony seems a bit sour for some reason on the yawing boat ride back to the house.

Greta, Scott, and Bertram spend the afternoon productively

diving for lobster and catching bottomfish. They bring back seven lobsters, three triggerfish, and fourteen snapper, almost all of which we grill and eat with fish cakes Greta makes from the remaining snapper, a soup Patricia makes from chicken bones, pasta, a salad, and a brilliant Becky Gray hollandaise. Our gourmandizing anyway is still on a high plane, and is a solace.

Patricia comes to bed delightedly happy and finds me glum. She has spent her day sketching, picking flowers, gathering shells, and reading books on tropical fish. With no particular agenda here, since she rarely cares to fish, she is truly enjoying the journey, just as I counseled her to do. One definition, I decide, of a good, do-it-yourself fishing destination is that it is a place where everything that can go wrong can do so and yet some (perhaps simpleminded) member of your party with low to no expectations will still feel that he or she is on vacation.

Tuesday, March 16. Weather desperate again—no light and a raging wind, now from the east, that seems determined to wreck us from every point of the compass.

Basically, we sit around all day. Ed and Becky do a little digressive trolling in the morning: one 'cuda strike. Tom takes more pictures of stormy weather and all of us sitting around. Tony gone; Outrage part not here; and Bertram's younger brother's boat running rough. Everyone still having fun, though—all glasses here still proudly half-full.

In the afternoon, Tricia, Greta, Scott, and I go snapper fishing with Bertram in a heaving sea. I show them my special, tried-and-true bottom-fishing technique of lifting the bait just off the bottom and jigging it, but somehow we catch fewer fish than they did yesterday.

Good fish-cake sandwiches for lunch. Bertram fries some barracuda for dinner. We are out of wine.

After dinner we try out titles for a magazine story I am obliged by contract to write about our experiences here. "The Curse of the Mellowtating Bonefish" is one. "Jerome's Revenge," is another—Jerome being a friend of ours whom we were forced to bump from coming along on this trip.

Wednesday, March 17. The worst weather yet! Gale-force winds out of the southeast, electrical storms, and astonishing amounts of rain. It's like being locked in the movie *Key Largo* with no way out.

A status report on the fishing prospects: Tony is gone again; we haven't seen him in two days. His seventeen-foot Whaler is here, but it now has a hole in the bottom, making it useless; the Outrage part has not arrived and I'm convinced never will; and the boat belonging to Bertram's younger brother is now completely on the blink and also unusable. In short, we no longer have any way to fish: so much for that. We are grateful, however, that there are still many pleasurable options left to us.

The highlight of the morning was watching the cat eat a baby chicken and then go pee in Ed's suitcase all over his tackle. I asked Greta if she thought *that* was an omen.

She and Scott have to leave this afternoon to spend the night at Peace and Plenty in order to make their early-morning flight to Fort Lauderdale tomorrow—if, that is, we can figure out how to get them off the island. Poor Scott has not exactly had the trip he envisioned when he spent $300 on bonefish flies back in Jackson Hole. As for Greta—I will no doubt hear her impressions of the fishing in the near future.

This afternoon Patricia, Greta, and I take a little family walk around the island to appreciate some of its subtle, unexpected pleasures. I fall through a piece of weak coral and badly carve up my left leg. Have to use my photogenic bandana to stanch the bleeding, then find a stick for a cane to hobble back to the house.

Phone here is permanently down, but somehow Bertram shows up in still another boat in time to get Greta and Scott back to Exuma before dark. The rest of us stand on the dock in the pouring rain waving good-bye, suspecting that the kids will be miserable at Peace and Plenty tonight after their do-it-yourself fishing adventure, but wishing them well. We have little food left, and no milk or bread. But it doesn't matter, since no one is much in the mood to cook anyway. We imagine Greta and Scott in the bar at Peace and Plenty, having to put up with all that forced lodge gaiety, then going into the very good little restaurant overlooking pretty Elizabeth Harbor and having to order a meal . . . and we feel, well, a twinge of sympathy for them.

Tom and Bertram go out late with flashlights to capture and photograph three big gray land crabs. We put them in a bucket with some food to sustain them, as we may very well have to eat them.

Thursday, March 18. We can't fish, of course—haven't been able to for days. Nor can we snorkel or swim in the cold, wind-whipped water. My leg, which may be infected, is too sore to go looking for any more unexpected pleasures the island might hold, but we have two days left here. Luckily, Patricia and I remember when we wake and stare up at the chameleon on our ceiling, wondering how we will get through the next forty-eight hours, that the beautiful sea and beach are still outside and can be looked at. So we go down to the dock and sit there in the rain and wind, looking at the sea and beach. The beach, we admit after a while, looks remarkably like a used handkerchief; and the sea is the poisonous milky blue of antifreeze—an interesting color, perhaps, but not exactly beautiful.

At breakfast Tom offers another title suggestion for my story: "Fishing for Godot."

At nine o'clock, Tony, our Godot, calls Bertram . . . *calls* (the phone, magically, is working again, and after Tony hangs up we all scramble to be the first to stick a finger in it and call *anyone*) and instructs Bertram to pick him up immediately in Barre Terre and deliver him to Clove Key. We have not seen Tony since Monday and wonder what he possibly could want. But he and Bertram never return, so we don't find out.

Over a fairly grim lunch made up of the last leftovers in the house, we decide that we are almost certainly part of a control experiment on deprivation response being conducted by Tony and his family for the University of the Bahamas psychology department. Of *course!* Why didn't we see it before? we ask ourselves. Take these simple, childlike Americans to Clove Key, Tony was obviously instructed, cut off the boats, the fishing, the phone, the wine, and finally the food, and let's see what shakes out. Patricia even points out that the sophisticated methodology of the Outrage—continuing to dangle it day after day as a possibility—is classic child psychology. Determined to meet whatever fate awaits us at the end of the experiment as calmly as possible, we all take long naps after lunch.

At five-thirty, Bertram and one of his younger brothers pop over and drop off an unlikely load of groceries—lettuce, eggs, ice cream, cookies, and candy bars. It is, we see darkly, the sugar water in the rat's cage, the test-prolonging appeasement of sweets. But with no longer any culinary pride left, we eat it all anyway for dinner, washed down with the last of our vodka, and go to bed wondering what will become of us.

Friday, March 19. I realize before I open my eyes that something is radically different. I lie in bed and concentrate. There is no . . . *wind!* For the first time in a week there is no wind moaning and rattling over the house. I sit up and look outside: the palm fronds are still, and there is a splash of *sun on the deck!* I leap out of bed and shake Patricia, fairly slobbering with joy.

"It's over! They've called off the Clove Key Experiment— we've beaten them!"

"What?" Patricia says.

"The sun is shining. The wind is down. We're *saved*—we can fish," I shout.

Bertram appears at nine, a bit hung over, it seems. Tony, he says, is coming too, in his own now-repaired boat, and will be here within the hour. We wait on the dock, basking in a morning as perfect as a baby's toe, as soft as a catkin. And Tony *does* show within an hour in a grand mood, pointing out the glories of the day as if he had arranged for them, and maybe he had. Because of those very glories, no one can possibly be in a mood to say anything to him other than "Let's go fishing."

◆　　　◆　　　◆

So this is the strange truth about how we came to be on that gorgeous little bonefish flat described at the beginning of my story, at 11:00 A.M. on our last day in the Bahamas, just as the tide began to come in and with it hordes of bonefish. And here is further truth about what happened there.

As mentioned, we started wading the flat with the sun, breeze, and tide behind us, spotting bonefish in numbers. There was no good reason for them to be there on that flat, with the water still cold and discolored, but there they were . . .

Just as we had known they would be, really, when we sat up the night before planning our strategy for the next day. Anyway, now that there were finally fish within reach of our long rods, the three of us knew exactly what to do, and we did it. We picked the little flat clean, and then moved on to another one behind Barre Terre that Ed and I had chosen the night before for the clearing weather we knew was coming. As we stepped out of the boat, we could almost feel the lurking presence of Mister Bone. And as soon as we spread out and began walking the flat, we started picking up a school here, a pair of gorillas there. I put a cast to the second school I saw, dropping one of my secret Surething ties as soft as a whisper three feet in front of the lead fish. I let the fly sink and waited until the school was over it; twitched it once, twice; and then—I'll never know how this happened—*three* fish grabbed it at the same time and headed for Cuba . . .

THE CONVERSION

OF EPSTEIN

WE FINALLY LEFT THE DOCK AT COZUMEL AT 9:00 A.M. and were tossing around in the strait a thousand yards off the coast of Yucatán by ten. There was not a single trout angler in sight, and that was just fine with Epstein.

In fact there wasn't any kind of angler in sight, though this was May and the middle of the annual sailfish run. A thirty-knot wind was blowing, there were eight-to-ten-foot seas running in the strait, and nobody but José wanted any part of it. All those fifty-foot Strikers and Merritts and Hatterases sitting back there at the dock like a meeting of the board of directors of the Bass Weejun Company, and every one of their captains with something else to do today but fish. Including the guy Epstein and I had chartered: Emilio.

"Ees too windy. Maybe *mañana*," Emilio had said and gone back to cleaning the already spotless cabin of the fifty-two-foot Egg Harbor he captained. It belonged to a man from Pennsylvania—a trout angler, Epstein was sure, who had instructed Emilio never to go fishing when the wind was blowing.

I had reminded Emilio that we had to leave *mañana*, and also that neither Epstein nor I had yet caught a sailfish on a fly rod. That was what we had come down here to do, but for the past two days we had let Emilio and the wind keep us from trying, and had settled for catching sail after sail on twenty-pound trolling tackle. Today was our last chance.

"Good-bye," Emilio had said to that, and closed the cabin door.

◆   ◆   ◆

More seriously, it was fishing's last chance with Epstein. Epstein had given up fishing almost two years before. Until this week he hadn't touched a rod since a July afternoon when a long-simmering hatred for what he called "trout anglers" had finally boiled over.

We had been fishing emergers on a snobbish little brook in Vermont, the guest of George Talbot, a man I knew who was always talking about "riseforms" and his latest reading of Dame Juliana, but was otherwise, to my mind, okay. Not to Epstein's mind, however. He and Talbot had developed a strong antipathy for each other over the course of the two days we fished together, and I was much relieved at the end of the second day when it appeared that Epstein and I were going to get back to New Hampshire without any outright unpleasantness between the two of them.

Talbot and I had been taking down our rods, talking peacefully beside his car in the warm dusk with a bottle of Beam on the hood between us when Epstein came galumphing out of the brook, his forefinger stuck through the bleeding gills of a large brown trout.

"Look at this," he shouted to me. "Do you believe this fish came out of this pissant little stream?" He tossed the trout at our feet, where it pitched feebly a couple of times in the dust.

Talbot looked at the fish, then up at me, his face pale. "Do you intend to kill this lovely fish?" he asked Epstein without looking at him.

"You bet, pal," said Epstein happily. "Kill it and eat it."

"I'm sorry, but I have to ask that you let me measure it first."

"Be my guest," Epstein said proudly.

Slipping to his knees, Talbot pulled a retractable tape from his vest, straightened the fish and measured it. "She's not legal," he said. "We'll have to release her."

"What are you talking about?" Epstein demanded. "The limit is eight inches. That fish has to be over fifteen."

"Eighteen exactly," said Talbot. He was quickly constructing a little platform out of twigs. "I think she'll be okay if we can just get her back to the water without *touching* her anymore." He looked up at me, ignoring Epstein. "We have a regulation here that we only kill fish between eight and sixteen inches. Or, of course, anything over twenty inches . . ."

"*What?*" thundered Epstein.

"Of course, *most* of us haven't killed a fish of any size in years." Talbot slid the trout gently onto the little stretcher he had made, and stood up carefully. "I think she'll be all right, don't you?" he asked me.

"Well," I said, "it's bleeding from the gills."

"Let me get this straight," said Epstein weirdly. We were both following Talbot as he catwalked toward the stream, holding the trout stretcher gingerly aloft. "That fish is two inches too short to be legal, and it's also two inches too *long* to be legal? Is that right?"

"*Legal* isn't exactly the right word. It's just the way we all agree to do things here on the Passacowadee."

I hadn't liked the sound of Epstein's voice, so I said, "Look here, Talbot, I really *don't* think that fish is going to make it . . ."

Epstein interrupted me by suddenly hopping in front of Talbot and snatching the trout off the stretcher. "The way I see it," he said, looking from Talbot to me and back again, his eyes glittering, "we've got two classic trout angler problems here: Number one"—he held up the fish by its tail—"is this trout going to live or not? And, number two, he's two inches too long for those of us here on the Passacowadee."

Talbot wanted the trout back. He reached out for it, but he was too late, because just then Epstein stuck the fish's entire head into his mouth and bit down. Holding the tail with both hands, he gnawed away furiously, snorting and huffing like a grizzly, and spitting out trout blood and pieces of flesh, until finally he had chewed off the head—which he spat on the ground at the feet of the pale, hypnotized Talbot. Epstein grinned wolfishly. In his last civilized utterance of any kind to a trout angler, he had said in a deceptively kind voice, "You see how easy it is to solve these little problems if we just put our heads together?"

◆   ◆   ◆

Of course, it was not everyone who fishes for trout who drove Epstein to give up the primary passion of his life, but only that percentage (growing daily, he believed) who qualified in his mind as trout *anglers*. Epstein's trout angler had rules to govern every pleasure, and that was what Epstein most despised about him. But he also hated the fellow's stuffiness and academic bent, his pipe and tweed hats, how vulnerable he looked in waders, his sheepish enthusiasm for following other trout anglers, his womanish sentimentality, the prissy way he ate and drank, his physical cautiousness, and his obsession with minutiae: little flies, little rules, little tools hung all over his vest, the invention of little tactical problems to make trout fishing seem harder than it was.

In the last year or so before he quit fishing, Epstein had

begun to see trout anglers behind every bush and tree. In West Yellowstone and Ennis, in Maine and Idaho, in Labrador and Argentina, everywhere he went they were waiting for him, pursing their lips over some local rule, wading cautiously in shallow water with the help of a stick, making flaccid little casts, spooking fish they never saw, lighting their pipes, and talking sentimentally. Talbot was just a merciful last straw. When pushed, Epstein would acknowledge that Talbot was not the most egregious trout angler he had ever met, just the last; and he would even express some regret at having thrown Talbot bodily into the "Sundown Pool" of the Passacowadee.

But however good or bad his motives, Epstein had sworn off all fishing that day in Vermont, and not fishing began to ruin his life. His marriage and his medical practice fell into shambles. He began to drink too much, and he developed an unnerving habit of picking fights with anyone wearing a uniform.

I happen to enjoy the company of people who are actively engaged in wrecking their lives over something they like or don't like, so long as they are not members of my immediate family; but one night Epstein's wife took me aside at a party and asked me for help. She looked up at me with her great, dark, Byzantine eyes and pleaded with me to "do something." We rarely saw the Epsteins socially, and I was moved. So I talked him into coming down to Cozumel with me. He had never done any saltwater fishing, and I was sure he would take to it. For the first few days, though, he had found Emilio's pussyfooting about the weather, the cleanliness of his boat, etc., to be just another form of trout angling.

Fishing, it appeared, was about to lose Epstein permanently; and then we walked down the dock and met José.

◆   ◆   ◆

José was sitting in a rusty lawn chair in the stern of a dumpy, homemade-looking, thirty-foot boat called the *Gloria*. He knew no English and Epstein and I only little Spanish, but we worked out the essential details in a matter of minutes. Epstein and I were given to understand this clearly: we had found a skinny, barefoot Indian with a pot belly who didn't give a rat's ass how much wind was blowing.

The *Gloria* didn't have sonar or teak decks or a shower. Neither did she have a few more necessary accouterments to sport fishing—such as outriggers, a mate, or bait. But she did have an ice chest full of Dos Equis, and Epstein and I found a nice blue-skirted lure which we rigged without a hook on one of José's decrepit fifty-pound trolling outfits. As soon as we hit the straits, José turned up sea, cut the *Gloria* back to trolling speed, put on a Jimmy Buffett tape and—drinking beer with one hand and spinning the wheel with the other, laughing and singing to himself and hopping around like a potbellied parrot—commenced to go fishing.

At first Epstein and I couldn't stand up in the cockpit. But when we could, we let the lure out and sailfish started jumping all over it. Everywhere we looked behind the transom, there were sailfish, herds of them, lit up and running over each other to get to the lure. I gave Epstein the fifty-pound outfit and lurched toward the cabin for my fly rod.

"They're trying to eat the goddamned thing," Epstein shouted after me. All either of us knew about fly-fishing for billfish was what we had read.

I staggered back into the cockpit holding the fly rod and shouted, "Just don't let them cut it off, it's the only lure we've got." Epstein was crouched at the transom, his knees locked under it, whipping the boat rod up and down and making the blue lure leap and plunge thirty yards back. Through the waves we could see sailfish diving and jumping all around it. I tried false-casting and couldn't because of the wind, so I dropped the big red-and-white steamer into the prop wash and let the boat's momentum carry it back about fifteen feet.

"I'd better go tell José what to do," said Epstein. "Here." He shoved the boat rod over to me. "I'll tell him to throw the boat out of gear when I shout."

"How are you going to tell him that?"

"Small, small problem, amigo," said Epstein. "About the size of a trout angler's dick."

While he was gone, the boat quartered into a particularly big sea, yawed, and crashed into the following trough. Behind me I heard glass shatter and Epstein curse, then he was beside me again at the transom, grabbing back the boat rod.

"José is all set. I'm going to bring this lure in, so get ready and don't blow it."

I pulled the tip of the fly rod up into the wind to my right as far as I could without lifting the streamer off the water. Then I stripped some line off the reel and onto the deck, and hoped I could make one good cast. Epstein was reeling fast, and the blue lure skipped toward us, hounded by sailfish. When the lure was about fifty feet away and still coming, Epstein said, "You ready?"

I nodded.

"*José!*" Epstein yelled, and just as the boat went out of gear, he yanked the boat rod up and backwards over his head, lifting the lure off the waves and catapulting it toward us. Confused, the sails milled thirty feet off the transom. I lifted the fly rod's tip another inch or two and pushed it hard forward. The streamer picked up, caught the wind, and rode it out perfectly to the sailfish, pulling loose line off the deck. When it slapped down I started stripping it back in foot-long jerks. The streamer hadn't traveled a yard before a sailfish charged in a quick, silver furrow of water and ate it. I let go of the underside of the transom with my knees, reared back to hit the fish, and slipped. Epstein caught me and held me upright. "Hit the fucker again," he said, and I did, three times, and then we watched the backing pour off the reel.

"Why is there blood all over the deck?" I asked Epstein.

"A window broke in the cabin and I cut my leg on it."

"Isn't that an awful *lot* of blood?"

He was still holding me upright against the transom while I played the fish, and I could feel blood running down the backs of my legs.

"It's okay, just don't lose that baby. Can you *believe this?*" he whooped. The sail was tail-walking a hundred yards back, its lean, violet body snapping like a flag in the wind. "We have wasted our whole *lives* fishing in mudholes for guppies. I have just been made *whole*, goddammit . . .

"I have to puke now," he added after a moment. His voice was still so delighted I thought he was kidding. He wasn't. Without letting me go, he turned his head and threw up violently onto his shoulder and the deck. When he was finished, he coughed a couple of times and spat. "Deep-sea fishing!" he shouted hoarsely into my ear. "To hell with women and work!"

With Epstein holding me upright and with José handling the boat beautifully, I had the sail tired and circling just off the stern in eight minutes. When the fish moved under the boat, I yelled for José to go forward. Taking me to mean the fish was ready, I guess, he threw the boat into neutral and popped back into the cockpit like a jumping bean, gloved for billing the fish and thrilled to death with everything that was going on, even, it appeared, the unexplained blood and vomit all over his deck.

"*Go forward!*" I yelled to him and pointed to the fly line running directly under the stern, which at that moment stopped and refused to budge. The fish had run the line around the prop.

"Oh no," Epstein said quietly, and let me go.

"Aiyeee!" said José. He popped back into the cabin, reemerging in seconds in a mask and fins and, before Epstein or I could figure out what he was doing, jumped overboard into the heaving sea.

Epstein and I looked at each other, then overboard. It was not a place *anyone* would have wanted to be. Between the fish and the fly line was a foot of sixteen-pound leader tippet. Though we didn't say it, neither Epstein nor I believed that the tippet had not already parted, either on contact with the prop or at the fish's first surge. But within seconds the line came unstuck and I felt it to be, miraculously, still connected to the fish.

Epstein pulled José back into the boat and José got the engine going and the boat turned upwind, then he came into the cockpit and grabbed the sailfish by its bill. He pulled the fish half over the transom, and Epstein started clubbing its electric-blue head with a Coke bottle.

"Stop it," I said to him. "That's my fish, and I want to release it." Even before I had finished the sentence, I was sorry I had spoken it.

Epstein paused with his hand raised, and looked at me. His face was set with a fierce new assurance, and his eyes had the same noncommittal savagery in them that you sometimes see in animals' eyes.

"The hell you say," he said quietly. Then he clubbed the fish again with the bottle and José let it slide dead onto the deck.

Both of them straightened up then, and grinned at me. Epstein had tied his T-shirt around his thigh, which had finally stopped bleeding. In real life he is a doctor, but he doesn't look much like one. He is also an ex–college football player and wrestler, an enthusiastic fistfighter and skydiver—a big, hard, trouble- and pain-addicted man. Later, back in Cozumel, not trusting Mexican clinics, he would disinfect and sew up his wound himself. It took thirty-five stitches to close the cut, and then we went out and drank a world of Cuervo Gold and said very little to each other.

One thing Epstein did say, late that night, was that he had found his religion. He said this very loudly at about three in the morning while staring unsteadily at a stuffed blue marlin hanging in the lobby of our hotel. And I suppose I believed him.

I have not seen Epstein since that trip, but occasionally I hear about him and his fishing. My friend Captain Bob Marsten wrote me recently that he and Epstein took a Striker, a Morton's salt box of cocaine, and two hookers down to Chile this past winter to look for swordfish, but spent all their time shooting sharks and getting laid in the tuna tower.

I have learned for a fact that very little in life is simple, even fishing. But there for a moment or two in the cockpit of the *Gloria*, standing astride his sailfish, shirtless and hairy, new-looking and sweating and caked with dried blood and puke, Epstein was, I believe, a simply happy man. After he had grinned at me for a long time, he picked José up and hugged him. Then he sat the little Indian carefully back down on the deck.

"Muchas gracias," Epstein told him.

José ran up to the wheel, cracked a *cerveza*, turned up the Buffett, and winked at us over the stained shambles of his boat. He put the throttle in the corner and the *Gloria* heaved forward. "More fish now, *si?*" he shouted.

Epstein squinted approvingly at him. "I'd say . . . a hundred and sixty-four, maybe one-sixty-five."

"What's that?" I asked him.

"Trout anglers that little bastard's worth."

FISHING FOR GRACE WITH THE BLACK DOG IN THE LAND OF PONCE DE LEÓN

S O THERE I WAS, FETCHED UP IN KEY WEST AFTER FIFTEEN straight days of fishing, sunburned, a blister on my casting hand, and the black dog still on my trail. The black dog had been following me around for months. Maybe you've been there: where if you didn't have bad luck you wouldn't have any luck at all; where your life looks to you like the workbench in a small engine repair shop; where you're angling hard for answers, not missing a cast, but your fly got snapped off in a willow tree an hour before and you don't know it yet. A lot of people in Key West on any given day have been there too, some of them for so long it's made them a little silly in the head. But this guy didn't look like one of those.

I was turning in to a coffee-and-bagel place on Simonton Street when I first noticed him walking down a side street a couple of blocks away, wearing shorts, a backpack, and a straw hat, and carrying a staff ornamented with buckskin. He looked jaunty and purposeful, and something made me want to see him up close, but he was headed away from the restaurant, so I went on in and broke my fast.

When I came out a half hour later, the man fell into step beside me on the sidewalk as if he had been waiting for me, and we immediately began to talk as naturally as if we were resuming a conversation we had carried on for years. I saw that he wore a handsome necklace of claws with a leather packet in the center. He was of medium height and build, tidy and animated.

Did he live here, I asked him. No. Where? Everywhere, he said. He had come here from Boulder. He came and went according to God's will, and God told him where to go with signs. He had just that morning been given a sign to go on to Albany, New York, which meant that whatever it was he was here in Key West to do was nearly done. He spoke very well, with a strange but pleasant accent that was perhaps Middle Eastern. In the five-block walk in the hot sun down Simonton Street to the green gate of my hotel, he said a lot without seeming to hurry, and it was clear he was talking directly to me.

He had been homeless for seventeen years, he told me, and that was as he wanted it, since it was only through dispossession that we own and keep our power. *What?* I thought—I, who had recently somehow misplaced my own, such as it is, couldn't find it anywhere, and had prayed for clues the very night before in my hotel room at the bottom of the continent—"You have to do *what* to keep your power?"

"Give things up, number one, and recognize that everything is fine. We try to plan, we want things. Someone tells you to do something. None of it matters. We belong to God. He makes everything possible, controls everything. Relax. Everything is just fine."

He said something about following a cloud; something about Lucifer. At one point I was moved to tell him he was lucky, and he corrected me: he was blessed; luck had to do with other things. When we stopped in front of my hotel, I asked

him his name in a voice cracked with . . . what? Longing? Inti-
mation? He turned around and looked at me for the first time
and Ohh, *Son!* the *face*—the soft curls of hair around it, the
beard, the worn, resilient kindness in the eyes. The face was an
icon; where had I *not* seen that face before? His old name, he
said, was Samuel. His new name was Jesus.

All I could manage to do was give the guy five dollars, all the
money I had on me, and croak that I wanted to buy him lunch.
Then I handed him a bottle of grapefruit juice I was carrying
and told him I hoped it provided him with a cool drink on his
way to Albany.

He held up the bill. "There is a bank in heaven we all draw
on. I had wanted to go to Burger King for breakfast and now
here is my way to do that. And I have a drink for the road, too.
Heaven is here," he said. "We misunderstand heaven."

My face twitching, knowing without question I was experi-
encing something I couldn't explain, I shook his hand and said,
"God bless you." Then I went into my little hotel room and
cried like a baby and wondered if I was going crazy or having
some kind of breakdown caused by too much fun in the sun.
After a while I sat up on the side of the bed and said, "Okay.
Okay, fine." And in a few minutes more I was ready to get on
with the hard labor that fishing had become for me over the
past couple of weeks.

We misunderstand heaven indeed.

◆　　◆　　◆

The idea had been to start at the top of Florida and fish to the
other end, casting as wide a net as possible in just under three
weeks. Photographer Tom Montgomery and I had performed a
similar road-angling exercise in Montana nearly two years ear-
lier, and that trip had been a spirited, movable feast of friends

coming and going, memorable encounters, meals and lodgings, with some very good fishing serving sort of to cleanse the palate between courses. We would sally forth to feast again, thought Tom and I, this time on the nearly limitless angling possibilities of Florida in the month of May—with other pilgrims, with carefree hearts, with the insatiable appetite of skill . . .

And this time, too, as it turned out, with the yapping black mutt that had lived underneath my bed all winter.

At first Jimbo Meador believed the dog was his, but I knew all along the ugly scoundrel was mine and it was just pissing on Jimbo's tires. It started doing that right out of the gate. Tom and I had just arrived in the happening little town of Apalachicola, driving down from Tallahassee in a rented Gulf Stream blue Chevrolet Lumina, and were having a drink in the convivial bar of the Gibson Inn when Jimbo called to say his car had blown a gasket in Pensacola. It was about 6:30 P.M., the first day of the trip; the dog hadn't even unpacked yet.

Jimbo talks like Forrest Gump, which is not surprising since that fictional character—created by Winston Groom, one of Jimbo's closest friends—was partially inspired by him (the non-idiot part, Jimbo would point out), and since Tom Hanks studied Jimbo's voice to prepare for the role. As far as I'm concerned, Jimbo should be studied by *all* movie actors and other impressionable young people, and not just for his voice. In fact, he ought to be a mandatory course called something like "The True and Vanishing Southern Gentleman and All-Around Outdoorsman 101."

As a regional business manager for the Orvis Company, part of Jimbo's job is fishing, and much of that fishing is done in north Florida. He had organized the first three destinations of our trip, and had volunteered his vehicle, a nineteen-foot

Hewes tunnel skiff, and his own self to go along with Tom and me for at least the first week. A Jimbo breakdown was serious bad news.

"Don't worry," he told me over the phone. "We'll figure something out." I found that advice easier to take than it might have been, since Happy Hour at the Inn had gone into fifth gear.

On the big front porch of the Gibson, the drink-carrying men and women were all nice looking and had smug, in-on-the-ground-floor looks on their faces. Circulating in the bar around a bouncy piano were ruddy-cheeked men with red suspenders, Rolexes, and ponytails, and women in tight shorts and Lily Pulitzer green and yellow. Tom and I took our solace among them for a while, and then in the excellent dining room. And in the night, sure enough, Jimbo arrived with the skiff but no car.

And so did another of our group, my old friend Bob Carlson, M.D., stumbling into the room we shared around 2:00 A.M., his customary six to eight hours late. I turned on the light and watched him arrange his black Ninja throwing knives on the table between our beds and put his brass knuckles and .38 Smith & Wesson in the drawer. Carlson has a strong antipathy toward becoming a victim of violence.

"The fishing's going to be great," he told me. "I feel lucky."

In fact, the fishing over the next two days was the best Tommy Robinson had seen in more than three months; and for a few hours on the second day, the sight fishing for tailing redfish was the best he had *ever* seen, a fact that wound up causing him as much frustration as joy since he was guiding Carlson, me, and the black dog.

Robinson was a colorful, highly regarded flats guide in Key West from '78 to '88, then a corporate pilot in Alabama and then a pilot/guide for a fly-out bonefishing operation in the Bahamas. In 1995 he made an inspired move to Apalachicola, starting a guiding business with his brother Chris and getting his real-estate license just as the values of property and sport-fishing began to appreciate. Now he can equip you with tackle out of his family-owned Orvis shop, guide you expertly, and then sell you the house you will probably want to buy after sampling the wonderful fishery he has practically to himself.

In the Apalachicola River are bass and bream; offshore are king mackerel, cobia, amberjack, grouper, and snapper, and inshore, on the endless flats of Apalachicola and St. Joe Bays, are pompano, jack crevalle, speckled sea trout, and redfish. Owing to spectacularly successful conservation measures initiated within the past decade in the state of Florida, the latter two species are there now in numbers and sizes that haven't been seen in years. We spent our two days with Tommy Robinson in St. Joe Bay, without another boat in sight even though it was a weekend, covered up in redfish and specs. But yea, though there were fishes everywhere, I either cast my line into the sea and caught not or I hooked up and boated not.

Tom Montgomery fished with Jimbo. Carlson and I were in Tommy's boat, a slick sixteen-foot Aluma Weld johnboat with a thirty-horsepower engine and poling platform. Up at Cape San Blas on the first day—a cloudless, windless, baby blue wet dream of a fishing day—we found big schools of redfish on perfect white sand flats just off a sugary beach. It was precisely what we were there for—sight fishing for tailing and cruising redfish. In that pursuit, as in bonefishing, you stand on the bow, fly rod in hand, line stripped out onto the deck, while your guide poles the boat and both of you look for fish as if for a cure for AIDS. It is a method of angling I know a little something about, having spent a ludicrous amount of my life practicing it, and I enjoy believing I am competent at it: a dinky little pride to own, perhaps, but a comforting and longstanding one that rarely leaves me feeling as I do after I rollerblade with my daughter.

I caught *one* of the maybe two to three hundred redfish we saw on the flats that day, and so did Carlson. And Tommy Robinson, who is by nature a good-humored, chatty sort, seemed a bit wrung out and thoughtful on the run back in.

The next day he kept telling Carlson not to reel the leader into the tip of his spinning rod before he cast. Carlson—an ex–college football player and wrestler with a temper and a fondness for weapons, to whom pain, both received and inflicted, is an old friend—just looked at him and smiled.

Possibly Robinson's attitude was a bit abrupt because he badly wanted a photograph of one of the big redfish we kept encountering, tailing or following rays across the turtle grass flats of St. Joe Bay, and Carlson and I were not helping out. I managed to hook the first one we saw, a fish of about fifteen pounds, and the fly pulled out of its mouth after two long runs. Then Carlson lost a couple on his spinning rod. Then I hooked two real lunkers in a row and gave the fly rod to Carlson so that he could fight the fish, but he was not accustomed to a direct-drive fly reel and broke both fish off. Then I hooked another monster and the fly pulled out of *its* mouth . . . There were big, hungry redfish feeding everywhere, their tails winking impertinently at us in the sun: Tom and Jimbo were catching them, but Carlson and I never put one in the boat.

At one point I turned around to look at our captain and noted to myself that it was the first time I had ever actually seen anyone tearing his hair. "Don't reel the goddam leader into the *tip anymore*," he shouted at Carlson. "I've been fishing all my life and I *have never reeled the leader into the tip one time*. You've done it at least forty times just *today*."

Happily, Carlson was too engaged in the idiot's fun he and I were having not catching fish to take offense; and later in the day he redeemed himself by catching a trophy six-pound yellow-mouthed speckled trout. I was already beyond redemption, knowing for certain now that the dog was along for the ride and that it was going to be a long trip.

At the sublime Boss's Oyster House that night, where the motto is "Shut Up and Shuck," where the oysters are fixed in thirty different ways, where you hear people say things like "My friends call me Skeeter" and "I'm fixin' to shoot pool with one eye," I also heard someone say, "I might cain't grow old gracefully in this business," and I knew exactly what the man meant.

◆　　　◆　　　◆

Tom and I drove east on the nearly deserted two-lane Highway 98 to Perry, and then south on 98/19 through old Florida towns like Athena, Tenille, and Shamrock, over the Sewannee River, through shaggy green country of pines, palmettos, and moss-bearded live oaks, past mom-and-pop seafood stores, old boats beached in sandy front yards, and broken-down pickups with cast nets in the beds, to Weeki Wachee—the geographical center of the state.

Jimbo was supposed to be right behind us, towing the Hewes with a borrowed truck. When he hadn't shown up in three hours we went to dinner. On a television in the bar of the restaurant I watched the black, canine-toothed weather symbol for a cold front closing down on Homosassa Bay, where we were supposed to fish for tarpon the next day. And when we got back to the motel we learned that Jimbo was broken down again up the coast, this time with frozen trailer bearings.

Exhausted maybe from overwork, the dog took the next day off and stayed in the motel out of the rain and wind while Tom and I and Jimbo (on only two or three hours of sleep) went alternative fishing with Captain Mike Locklear, president and secretary of the Homosassa Guides' Association. The annual throngs of migrating tarpon had not yet shown up in Homosassa Bay, though they were expected any time, and the cold front had shut down other saltwater options. So Mike Locklear took us to the jungly, peat-colored Chassahowitzka River, lush with white spider lilies and bird life, and we had a lovely, pointless, and dogless time there, fishing like boys from rented canoes for bass and red-breasted sunfish.

As the man said, we misunderstand heaven, and the following day we were fishing with purpose again. Mike took us out in the bay on the clear, breezy tail end of the front, looking for cobia following rays on the flats. Both Tom in Jimbo's skiff and I in Mike's found a few and cast to them, and when they wouldn't even look at the fly, much less eat it, no one was surprised but Mike.

Fishing guides have different ways of dealing with angler adversities that can range, in my experience, from breaking a client's inneffective rod in two and stomping it into the deck of the boat to deeply ambiguous silences. Mike was a soothing, anecdotal man, and as the unhungry cobia were followed by more refusals from a sheepshead, a jack, and a redfish, and then, after a change of flies, by hooking up with first one good redfish and then another, only to have them both spit the hook on tight lines, he only murmured, "Bad luck," and went on with his story.

But that night at dinner he told a tale that seemed somehow, in my mounting anxiety, to resonate with metaphorical comment. A burnt-looking friend of his named Ken, whom we had met on the dock that morning, had gone away to the navy and wasn't the same when he came back. Now Ken owned practically nothing but a Labrador retriever and dozens of self-inflicted scars, acquired because he had come to enjoy cutting himself with a knife. The other day, said Mike, Ken had gotten into a fight and when his opponent pulled a knife on him Ken had grabbed it away and began cutting himself rapturously with it, sending the other man fleeing like a spooked redfish.

◆   ◆   ◆

As Tom and I pushed on south through more backroad old Florida, we passed a pickup near Hill 'N' Dale that advertised its owner as a "Christian Equine Podiatrist"; and then, in the traffic of Tampa, an aged van with a pop-up top and a hand-lettered sign taped to the back window that read "Two Teepees, Looking for Squaw," and gave the address and phone number of the driver, a shirtless Native American in his sixties or seventies with a hard face that gazed out, as contemptuous as Osceola's, at the passing Cadillacs from Michigan and the Busch Gardens billboards. Up there among those billboards the new Florida advertised its smug, avaricious self with a picture of traffic stuck in a snowstorm in some bleak northern clime and the words "We Know Where You're Coming From."

About two hours south of Tampa on Gasparilla Island is the town of Boca Grande, where the residents may know where you're coming from but couldn't care less. A peaceful, low-rise bastion of old money and old Florida pacing and reserve, Boca Grande is still not above claiming to be the tarpon capital of the world and, officially, tarpon were what we were there for. Privately, I was there at least as much for the emollients offered by the Gasparilla Inn, one of the state's best resort hotels and a place of great old-fashioned character and comfort. After checking in to a cottage there, Tom and I went fishing, and Jimbo, who had arrived without incident this time, spent the afternoon on the phone trying to straighten out the mess this trip had made of his life.

The tarpon fishing Boca Grande is best known for happens in midsummer in the deep water of the passes and is done using jigs or live bait. But from late April/early May through June, tarpon can also be found, sometimes in astonishing numbers, traveling and rolling on the surface of the Gulf from just off the beaches to four or five miles out, and these can be fished for with a fly rod. Which is what we intended to do, until we learned, with little surprise, that these "beach fish" were almost, but not quite, there yet. They were in Fort Myers, said Lew Morgan, and should move on up any day: the water temperature needed to be eighty-two degrees; it was now eighty-one.

So Lew took Tom and me fishing that afternoon for redfish and snook in the backcountry of Charlotte Harbor. Within the first dozen casts I hooked a big redfish by a mangrove island, pulled him out from under the roots, and fought him for a full five minutes before this one came unstuck. Lew glanced at me a little strangely when I told Tom that things were looking up. A little while later I even managed to bring a little snook all the way into the boat before a squall came up out of nowhere and drove us in.

After searching all the next day for tarpon along the beaches and not finding any, Jimbo's friend, the renowned Boca Grande tarpon guide Phil O'Bannon, told us they would probably arrive the next day, the day we had to leave—Jimbo to go home and Tom and I and the dog on to further angling misadventures. It was a shame we had to leave, he said, because when the fish first got there they were generally hungry. And plentiful: he had seen, he said, one hundred acres of tarpon rolling off the beaches. And easy: every cast could sometimes be a hookup.

It was a turn of great good luck at last, I decided, that I would avoid the opportunity of losing so many fish. But if the dog appeared to be easing up on me, he raised his leg one last time on Jimbo, who discovered just before he left that his five-hundred-dollar graphite composite push pole had been lost or stolen off the boat.

Or maybe buried like a bone.

◆   ◆   ◆

Only a short way out of Naples, headed south on the Tamiami Trail, the state goes suddenly from condo-user-friendly to impenetrable palmetto thickets, sawgrass barrens, and twisting, mosquito-clouded waterways, and even at sixty miles an hour it is clear why Osceola could be captured only by a U.S. Army deceit.

Everglades City is very old Florida. Maybe too old. I spent a few runaway months there writing an epic poem when I was seventeen, and the place is just as tatty and forlorn now as it was then. At the languorous old Rod and Gun Club, where Harry Truman dedicated into existence the Everglades National Park in 1949, a group of owl-eyed fishing guides and their clients were celebrating the conclusion of a three-day fishing tournament. As Tom and I ate dinner, we watched the awards being presented. "Most unusual fish" went to Arlene someone, with cute legs, for her flounder. She came up laughing adorably and said the trophy was bigger than the *feeish*. Then Bobbie Sutter won biggest redfish. She walked up to get her trophy looking sheepish, but flashed me a defiant expression when she caught me staring at her, perhaps mistaking my envy for lust.

The next morning we met guide Pete Villani and his friend Mike McComas at the dock on Chokoloskee Island, a tiny jump-off for fishing the Everglades and the Ten Thousand Islands that has become the place to be *du jour* among fed-up Keys guides and other Florida fishing cognoscenti. In Pete's Silver King and Mike's johnboat, carrying enough gear and food for two and a half days and two nights in the Glades, we ran an hour and a half from Chokoloskee to the Rodgers River chickee. Built in the water on pilings by the Park Service as one of a number of managed camp sites throughout the Everglades, the chickee was two wooden roofed platforms about eighteen by twelve feet, connected by a walkway with an outhouse in the middle, twenty-eight nautical miles out in the largest roadless wilderness and second largest national park in the United States.

We unloaded the gear and set up two tents on one of the platforms, saving the other platform for cooking and eating. Then, with a bit of eagerness for a change, I rigged up my fly rod. Exhilarated by the winding ride out through the mangroves, the alligators and rolling manatees we had passed, the herons and wood storks and white pelicans we had seen, and the flawless and luxuriant isolation of the chickee, I felt renewed and recharged, and even hopeful that we had given the dog the slip.

When we returned to the chickee that evening after fishing, the question of the dog's whereabouts was still up in the air. Sure, I had broken off a monster snook of maybe fifteen to eighteen pounds and had another one come unhooked, but I had also released a small snook and Tom, fishing in Mike's boat, had caught a seven-pounder that we kept to dine on. Casting into the mangroves with conehead streamers and blabbermouth poppers and seeing the snook flash out in the dark water for the flies like yellow, black-striped lances had been wonderful; and back at the chickee, after a swim, with a gin and tonic and a Cuban stogie, watching Pete expertly cook snook fillets and linguine with clam sauce as the sun made a florid exit from a cloudless sky, I had almost come to believe the dog was gator bait.

Then during dinner I stood up from the table to get a napkin and knocked one of Pete's two Coleman lanterns (this one borrowed) off the nail it was hanging from, totaling it. Just an accident, right? Too bad, no problem, sweep up the mess and go on with the stories, the eating, the camaraderie. But an hour later I stood up again to get something and destroyed the *other* lantern. This time there was nothing but deep silence. I could feel Tom and Pete and Mike staring at me in the dark. I went to bed.

Tom told me later that after a long silence following my departure, Pete had finally said, "Jesus Christ. It was like the guy was on some kind of *mission*."

Over the next day and a half, Tom and I had a wonderful time in great weather, in one of the world's most magical places and in the excellent, easy, and funny company of Pete and Mike. We ate, drank, and stogied very well and we caught plenty of snook and bass. But we did not catch a tarpon, and since just missing them in Homosassa and Boca Grande, I had gotten zealous about catching a tarpon on this trip. It is a fish I go back with; for forty years I have caught my share of them in various places around the world, and they have come easily to me when and where other fish have not. Because of that, I sort of consider the tarpon my grace fish and I was counting on it to pull me out of my slump—to give me back my missing touch and timing. If I could just catch a tarpon, I figured, spurning reason, everything would come right.

On our second morning I talked Pete into running a long way south and then into snaking up a tiny, mangrove-choked creek to a confluence where he had heard there were baby tarpon. I hooked a ten-pound snook there and, after pulling it out of the brush and over logs and unwrapping the leader from around the electric motor, almost lost it to a five-foot alligator, and would have except that Pete, who named the gator Wally, threw a plastic gallon water bottle at it and Wally took that off into the mangroves instead of my snook and loudly ate it.

Boating that snook and releasing it was surely a triumph over adversity, but it was not a tarpon; Wally, we figured—a dog in gator clothing, chewing up his plastic bottle back in the mangroves—had chased off all the tarpon.

The next day, our last with Pete and Mike, we did find tarpon but they wouldn't eat. In a creek leading into the lower Rodgers River there were tarpon rolling everywhere, and we all cast ourselves blind without scoring a bite.

Then we went into the Gulf and looked for snook for an hour or so over a green sand bottom.

I saw what I thought might be a fish. "Is that a fish?" I asked Pete.

"I'm not sure," he said. "Could be."

"Should I throw to it?"

"Hey, this is America," said Villani, who was raised in Michigan but sounds like he comes from Brooklyn, and who is fond of saying, "Hey, this is America."

I did and caught it. And then we headed back to Chokoloskee. It was a nice snook of six or seven pounds that jumped spiritedly, but it was not my grace fish.

◆   ◆   ◆

Country music leaks continuously out of every orifice of Roland Martin's marina, motel, condo, and tackle store resort complex in Clewiston, and bass boat trailers surround the place like lawn ornaments. In town as well as at the resort, there is no shortage of pictures of Roland Martin's tanned, smiling face, some of them bearing the inscrutable exclamation, "Ohh, *Son!*" Which is, Tom and I learned, what Roland Martin is given to saying when he is happily amazed, as in "Ohh, *Son!* What a hawg that bass was"—something he has probably said a lot as a legendary tournament bass fisherman and nine-time B.A.S.S. Angler of the Year. And since Martin is Clewiston's most famous son and bass fishing is second only to the U.S. Sugar Company as the biggest game in town, a lot of other citizens there probably say it too.

Surrounded by thousands of acres of flat, lime-green cane-fields, Clewiston is a pleasant, friendly, Little-League-and-fried-catfish kind of place that might be oppressively middle American were it not for a good number of resident Cuban sugar workers and their families, whose presence in town allows you to have a couple of bracing thimble-sized cups of sweet, strong Cuban coffee at the Farmacia while you wait for your Cuban sandwiches to take out fishing on the lake.

The lake there, of course, is none other than the voluptuous, fecund, funky-smelling Okeechobee, the great, south-tipped bowl whose drippings are the Everglades. At twenty-six miles wide and thirty long, comprising nearly 500,000 acres, Okeechobee is the largest natural freshwater lake completely within the borders of the United States. It is also one of the most productive bass lakes anywhere, and, with around a hundred guides working it, probably the busiest.

One of the best of those guides, a sleepy-eyed, slow-talking

James Dean lookalike named Danny Watkins, took Tom and me out on the lake's broad, glorious flanks for a few hours. We put in at the town of Moore Haven and ran a few miles down a canal past fragrant malaleuca trees and palms, with a few little lavender clouds in the early-morning sky and coots, egrets, and osprey on the wing, into Monkey Box Bay.

Danny is a "Hewes Celebrity Angler" and an Orvis-endorsed guide who used to compete in professional bass tournaments. As we drifted with the wind over beds of hydrilla and pepper grass, casting plugs and poppers and catching a bucketmouth here and there, he talked about competitive bass fishing: the $30,000 boats that top out at over sixty miles per hour, with their jackplates, automatically aerated live wells, depth finders that read sideways as well as vertically, metal-flake paint jobs, wall-to-wall carpeting, cellular phones, and color TVs. He talked about the new high-tech rods and reels; about spinner-baits, crankbaits, propbaits, buzzbaits, jerkbaits, rattletraps, and pigs-'n'–jigs; about flippin', pitchin', skippin', and jerkin' tech-niques. And then Danny Watkins smiled and said, "But you know, when you get right down to it, all a bass fisherman is is just a jerk waiting for a jerk."

On our way out of Clewiston, Tom and I stopped at Les's Saloon and Marge's Kitchen, a kickass porkchop sandwich, beer, and hotwings joint with apparent feminist sympathies. Signs on the wall over the pool tables remind you there are "So Many Men, So Few with Brains," and "A Husband Is Living Proof That a Woman Can Take a Joke." Up at the bar are pho-tos of some of the place's skydiver and biker clientele and the legend "If Assholes Could Fly, This Place Would Be an Air-port." As we drank beer and walked around the place, I read out loud to Tom another sign's sporting advice that "It's Not How Deep You Fish, It's How You Wiggle Your Worm."

"Now *that's* the truth," agreed one of the two been-there, done-that waitresses behind the bar—proving you never know in Florida where you'll run into a fellow angler.

One place where you can count on doing that consistently is along virtually any road in the state that crosses water. Tom and I drove up around the northwest end of the lake through Lakeport, Buckhead Ridge, and the town of Okeechobee, and in every pond and canal we saw, and from every bridge we crossed, there was someone fishing. On a bridge over Fish Eating Creek it was a black, retired Church of God minister named Reverend Charles Williams. Reverend Williams sat in a lawn chair, wearing tall green boots, a baseball cap, and a gold tooth, and tending two outfits: a cane pole and a spincast rod, both carrying ancient thirty-pound-test line and baited with worms—what the high-tech boys out on the lake probably called "dirtbaits."

Just off the bridge, the Reverend's wife Margaret sat in another lawn chair in the shade of their station wagon and watched him fish. Margaret had recently had a pacemaker put in her heart, and this was her first outing since the operation. She didn't fish: she had almost drowned once and had a fear of the water, and she didn't like to take fish off or bait hooks. But when the Reverend caught one, she would clean it and put it in the cooler in the back of their car, and she would cook it when they got home to Fort Myers, thirty-five miles away.

The Reverend was seventy-two and had been fishing all his life. Now that he was retired, he fished three days a week and sold vegetables on the other three. On Sundays he and Margaret went to Morrison's Cafeteria after church. Fishing relaxed him, he said. "But you got to have patience. You got to love it. *Love* it." He said Jesus knew about fishing. Then he told me the story about Peter, James, and John getting skunked. When they came ashore Jesus asked them how they did.

"They tell him they been trollin' all *day* and haven't caught nothin'. Jesus says, 'Go back to trollin', but fish on the other side of the boat.' They say, 'Oh no,' 'cause they tired of fishin', but at Jesus' command they launch into the deep again and then they caught such a multitude of fishes they had to get their pals to help 'em pull the net."

"'Fish on the other side,'" said the Reverend, looking up at me with a grin, his gold tooth winking. "That's what He told 'em. Maybe that's what I ought to do." But a moment later his spincast rod bowed and he started reeling without standing up. He asked me to look over the bridge railing to see what it was. "A gar," I told him as the fish started up out of the water, but then the frayed old line broke and it fell back in. That was just fine with Reverend Williams. A gar wasn't what he was after, though he would have taken it.

"I just like to feel the line pullin'," he said, laughing and tying on another hook. Margaret brought him a sandwich and a cup of lemonade and then went back to her chair.

"They not bitin' good yet," said the Reverend contentedly. It was just noon and he could stay until three, when he and Margaret had to drive back to the wholesale house in Fort Myers to pick up their vegetables for the next day. "But they will."

◆　　◆　　◆

If you believe the conventional wisdom that all of Florida is too crowded, try driving through the rodeo, barbecue, and gun-range country on Route 441 between Yeehaw Junction and Holopaw, where all you will see for miles is huge, palmetto-ringed pastures full of fat, heat-resistant cattle. Tom and I drove for twenty-six minutes on that road without seeing a car or a person; then, before we knew it we were in Satellite Beach and it was immediately clear where they had all gone.

Located just north of Melbourne, Satellite Beach is one of the dozens of East Coast strip towns whose high-rises and malls and fast-food restaurants run into each other all the way from Daytona Beach to Miami, forming an extruded, humid bazaar of services, goods, and amusements that is either your dream or your nightmare of modern Florida. Nowhere in all that crowded hawking would one expect to find an enormous, silent place of unpeopled white beaches and virgin oak hammocks with the cleanest water on the East Coast, miles of superb sight-fishing for redfish and speckled trout, and not a building in sight. But exactly such a place is Mosquito Lagoon, which is north of Cape Canaveral and the Space Center, and a part of Merritt Island National Wildlife Refuge.

Tom and I were guided there by Frank Catino, a city councilman for Satellite Beach and a well-respected light-tackle fishing guide. Frank's friend Ronny Winn joined us with his skiff, and rounding out our group was the redoubtable Paul Bruun, gourmand, raconteur, ace all-around angler, and trout guide from Jackson Hole, Wyoming. It seemed a formidable force of long-rod predators who sallied forth that day to battle the redfish of Mosquito Lagoon; but it was a chastened one that returned. Frank hoped that we could find, before anyone else did that morning, a dream school of close to two hundred redfish, each of them weighing between fifteen and thirty pounds, that he had found a number of times in the past few weeks loitering in a broad channel just offshore.

We did find them, almost immediately, and there wasn't another boat in sight. The sun was just right, the wind was light, and from the bow—as Frank poled me quietly up to what looked at a distance like an undulant, slowly moving, reddish brown carpet the size of half a football field—I thought, *Yes!* Here finally is redemption in spades! *Nobody* could screw this up, not even if the dog jumped in the water right now and . . .

"Cast," said Frank. I did, and stripped the fly past the pug-faces of at least ten redfish as long as your arm. Then I cast again . . . and again and again. The school continued to loll along on the top, unspooked, as I continued to cast into it, changing flies six times, praying cravenly after a while that I'd *snag* one. In Ronny Winn's boat, Paul Bruun was casting a spinning rod at the school and holding a plugging outfit between his knees. When the fish wouldn't eat one lure, he'd try the other one, then change them both. He and I beat the water to a froth, and the fish just mosied around our offerings, their dorsal fins wagging above the water at us like so many middle fingers.

But this utter rivening wasn't over yet. For the last ten minutes or so of our efforts, we were watched noncommittally by a shirtless, wired-looking young man in an old johnboat whom Frank knew to be a security guard at the Space Center. When Paul and I finally gave up, Frank invited the man to have a go.

"Naw, I don't want to screw up your fly-fishing," he said, somehow making that noble art sound like needlepointing. But when Frank told him we were leaving, he jumped into the bow and, with Frank directing him, poled upwind like mad to our school, using a piece of PVC pipe as a pushpole. Then he picked up a scrappy old spinning outfit, lobbed out a live mullet, and caught a fifteen-pound redfish.

We pulled over to his boat because Tom—believing now with irrefutable reason that it might be the last fish he would ever see with me in the boat—wanted a picture of it. The man had two big speckled trout and his one redfish limit for the day already on a stringer, so, after Tom had taken its picture, he let this one go. Watching the fish swim off, I felt a peculiar and unstable desire to shoot it with a deer rifle.

Impossibly, we went in that day skunked. All of us knew we had been under the spell of some powerful bad juju, but, like the farter in the elevator, only one of us knew where it came from. I basically gave up then. The next morning when Frank took Tom and me out early to a pretty little mangrove-lined canal off the Banana River where baby tarpon were rolling and sporting, I never even half expected one of them to eat the eight or nine different flies I threw at them. And fishing for them while they proved me right in that lovely place, on that lovely morning—felt like nothing so much as breaking rocks.

Later that day, Tom and I drove to Orlando, turned in our rented car with 1,527 fish-chasing miles on it, and flew to Key West. Abject and attenuated, I read an article on the plane in *Florida Sportsman* about the flathead catfish, and wondered if that might possibly be my next grace fish.

◆   ◆   ◆

After I had pulled myself together following the encounter on the street in Key West, I went to meet Tom at Faustus Grocery, "the oldest business in Paradise," to buy provisions for our trip to the Marquesas.

The Marquesas are the only atoll in the continental United States—a fifteen-square-mile collection of twelve uninhabited mangrove islands and hundreds of little islets circling a shallow lagoon. Lying twenty-five miles off Key West, the atoll is a part of the Key West National Wildlife Refuge, which status means no houses, no hunting, no seaplanes, no land-based camping. Though I have fished in the Keys since I was twelve years old, I had never visited the Marquesas, and I had badly wanted to for years, particularly after reading a well-water-pure little book called *Marquesa*, written by a man who spent six weeks in the summer of 1994 living alone on a small houseboat in the atoll's lagoon.

That man's name is Jeffrey Cardenas. He is an accomplished journalist, and has sailed a twenty-three-foot Ranger single-handed across the Atlantic. For nearly ten years he was one of the most skilled and sought-after flats guides in Key West, and now he owns a state-of-the-art fly shop, guide service, and guest house there. I liked his book and what I knew about him, so Tom and I called him a few months before our trip and he graciously offered to take us out to the Marquesas for a couple of days and nights on his houseboat. For him, it would be his first return trip to the islands on the boat since he wrote the book there. For us it was the highlight and last leg of the trip. For me it was, simply, now or never.

Tom and I met Jeffrey at the marina at Garrison Bight. We brought cigars, wine, rum, food, and water, and he brought lawn chairs, the last of the season's stone crabs, yellowfin tuna steaks, and shrimp. With his Maverick skiff in tow, we steamed out just after noon aboard the *Huck Finn*, a locally homemade job of twenty-six feet with a four-cylinder diesel capable of producing a meditative top speed of five knots. The houseboat had a bright, airy cabin about eight by twelve feet, with two bunks, a dining table, rod racks, a nice little galley, and a small open deck at either end. The roof of the cabin, with a Bimini-top shading the lawn chairs, served as a high, cool third deck.

I sat up there during most of the five-hour steam to the Marquesas, feeling better than I had in a long time. Jeffrey had told us that this was the first decent fishing day they had seen in three months. The wind had blown hard for ninety straight days and stopped the night before, and this was a sunny, light-breeze marvel of a day with more like it to follow. From the roof of the *Huck Finn*, floating like a cork over tan flats, feeling buoyant and in out of a long blow myself, I believed that maybe all of that good news was more than accidental. I wondered that I had let the man's hand go after I shook it; I wondered that I had not dropped to my knees there on Simonton Street and acknowledged publicly what I had felt was happening to me: that I was suddenly and inexplicably hooked up to a lunker answer or two, after half a year of blind casting. The answers were still not in the boat; I couldn't even identify them yet, and my recent record for losing what I stuck was not good. But at least I was playing something and the wind had stopped. And the black dog, I felt certain, was gone for good—left behind on the receding mainland.

By five-thirty, we had anchored the *Huck Finn* fore and aft in the lagoon and were drifting the northeast corner of the atoll in the Maverick, looking for tarpon. In two and a half hours we saw six or eight schools of rolling fish, some more than once. That was the good news. The bad news was that with all three of us casting to lots of fish, we could only get one to eat. And the worse news was that after Tom hooked it and handed me the rod so that he could take pictures, the heavy-duty handle of a brand-new Sage fly reel promptly sheared off in my fingers. For the first time in my life I experienced what is known as a cold sweat.

But back on the roof of the *Huck Finn* at sunset, it was hard to feel depressed. It was a perfect, all but dead-calm evening. Venus blazed, and there was lightning over the Everglades. Permit were tailing to the west, a shark was feeding just off the bow, and we were smoking Montecristos and drinking good rum. It was the trip's most accomplished single moment.

Though it had definite doglike nuances, I told myself, anything, after all, could cause the handle of a cherry five-
hundred-dollar fly reel to just break off in your fingers . . .

We ate asparagus, grilled tuna steaks with wasabi and fresh
ginger, and drank a bottle of Chardonnay. I took it as a good
sign that I didn't break a lamp after dinner. At ten-thirty, Jeffrey pulled his kayak off the roof and paddled off into the dark
with a fly rod to renew his personal relationship with the Marquesas. Tom and I went to bed. I lay on the bunk and hoped
hard that I would catch a tarpon the next day and catch it
gracefully, for my own pride and for the pride, too, of this nice,
dignified man who had brought us to this loved place and was
lending us the right to exploit it and trusting us to do that with
the proper respect of grace.

Yeah. Well, I'll spare you most of the ugly details, but what I
did, in fact, the next day was stink up the atoll. Wearing the
despicable stowaway dog around my neck like an albatross, I
didn't see fish until too late, lined them, threw at their non-
eating ends, and had them turn up their blunt noses at the fly
whenever I managed to get it in front of them. When I finally
did stick a little tarpon, *by accident*, he threw the hook on his
first jump.

Jeffrey didn't say much, as there was nothing much to say,
since you can hardly invite someone smelling up your boat in
the Marquesas to walk home. What he did do was twice take
the rod between my various boners and effortlessly, quite beautifully, catch a tarpon with it. I felt as coarse and slow and
clumsy as a mudhen flying alongside an osprey. At one point I
wanted to announce, "You know, I don't know what's going *on*
here, but I can usually *do* this. And what's more, I caught my
first tarpon on a fly rod the very year you were born . . ." but I
was afraid I'd start to drool or something and mess that up too.

To the Cherokee Indians, *a na su hv s gv* means "going fishing," and it is never a waste of time because it is an escape from self and goals and pressure—the exact opposite activity to, say, running for the United States Senate. Of all the good reasons in the world for going fishing, I decided that afternoon, not one should be to create or sustain a reputation for doing it well.

After another fine dinner, we took the skiff out "splooshing." We ran out to a finger channel between flats, and when Jeffrey cut the engine, the only light came from the crowded stars and the only sound at first was the subtle crablike clicking that mangrove islands make. Then we heard a sploosh. Then another, closer by—the sound of tarpon feeding in the channel on shrimp being washed off the flats by an outgoing tide. Casting a floating fly in the direction of the splooshes, Tom hooked up quickly and had a long, tough fight with a fish that finally sawed through the eighty-pound shock tippet. I lay on the bow looking up at the sky, delighted with this dry-fly fishing to slurps in the dark and delighted not to do it. I was tired not of fishing, but of my own poor, ego-hounded *self* fishing—and I was very happy just to lie there and listen to a fishing hole instead of trying to beat it half to death.

The next morning my back didn't hurt for the first time since Appalachicola. I was looking forward to going home that night and I didn't care anymore whether or not I grew old gracefully in this business.

It was maybe the most soothing morning I have ever seen, so still and uniformly lit when we first got up that there was no seam between the sky and the sea. Soon after we got out on the water in the Maverick, the sun came up through low clouds looking like a blood orange, turning the oily water mauve, and as it came up farther there was a dove-gray-and-mauve haze between water and sky, in which the islands of the atoll looked to be suspended. The sea took on a faint ripple, like a sheet just laid on a bed, and all around us was a blending of the palest blue and smoke gray, green, lavender, and turquoise, and through it pelicans dove, a skittering of bait flashed out of the water with a 'cuda or jack behind it, and a white heron stood ankle-deep on a flat, poised with one leg lifted.

On the north end of the islands, where Jeffrey rarely catches fish, we came onto a school of tarpon that was acres large, some of them rolling so close to us in the motionless sea that you could believe you saw expression in the great silver and black eyes. I cast to these fish over and over without a take. Then Jeffrey came down from the poling platform and jumped one, and when I took the rod again I found I could concentrate on putting the casts where they were supposed to go and yet not care what happened to them. I felt relaxed and divested, that everything was just fine, and that I was only doing something I love to do.

A little later, on the other side of the boat now, I cast again into the same school and the line came tight. I struck the fish with my line hand and felt that electric first connection with a wild thing that Jeffrey had said the day before was for him the defining moment of fishing.

And Ohh, *Son!* did that ol' tarpon jump then, rattling into the air and shaking himself like a dog passing peach pits. I felt the line pullin', as Reverend Williams had it, and knew what to do about it and how to do it, and knew, too, that this particular grace fish, this unsummonable gift, was already caught.

PART THREE

Rounding Third

E ARLY IN MY FIFTIES, PRAISE GOD, I WAS FINALLY caught and released. I started writing books again, and magazine articles on subjects other than fishing. I started traveling again quite happily with my wife to waterless destinations, and not caring very much anymore (most of the time) about the angling destinations I hadn't gotten to yet, or fishing from dawn until dark, or how many fish I caught. I started caring more about other things instead—such as the caretaking of angling resources.

During the blindered, hectic decade of my forties, I had been more or less unconscious to what was happening to the world's waters and fish stocks beyond how it might affect my fishing on a particular day. And becoming aware, toward the end of that decade, of how much had gone to hell in a hand basket felt like waking up to find your house has been burgled and painted with graffiti while you slept. For a while I went around saying out-to-lunch things like "What do you *mean*, the redfish were almost wiped out in the Gulf of Mexico? . . . That swordfish and bluefin tuna and Atlantic salmon are all headed the way of the moa? . . . That white marlin stocks have declined 86 percent worldwide since 1960?" Mercifully, I had friends who took the time to sensitize and educate me on these matters—Bill Taylor of the Atlantic Salmon Federation, Jody Bright, Karl Wickstrom, the people at the Louisiana Coastal

Conservation Association. Now, at least, I have a finger in that dike, and it will stay there until I die.

I also started caring about the people who fish for their lives rather than for sport, for whom fishing is the same as fate—who are as endangered a species in North America now as the Atlantic cod—and I spent time with those people on my home shore of Nova Scotia, in the Cajun country of Louisiana, and on the northwest coast of Newfoundland, where I passed some time in the rain hitchhiking after salmon, eating pickled sea bird, drinking black tea, and listening, in homes that had never seen electricity, to stories the Apostle Peter might have told.

I am both more and less demanding about my fishing now than I used to be. I prefer the company of children, old people, and the few nonchalant experts I know over the fanatics I used to sprint with. I no longer mind not catching fish, but I want to catch them or not on water I have some feeling for. I still love and practice fly-fishing, but increasingly I am going back to the whatever-it-takes, grab-bag angling that my father and I did together. I learned cast-netting, handlining, surf casting, and trotlining from him, and we trolled, minnow-fished, plug-cast, and bobbered with a worm or live cricket as often as we fly-fished. In the past few years I have enjoyed revisiting some of those methods. Coming back to them from the often parched, prissy, peacock world of fly-fishing makes them taste to me like a dipperful of spring water, exactly the same as they did when I first tried them.

My father was the most complete fisherman I've ever known. Second to him would be Paul Bruun, who does it for a living and with an indiscriminate curiosity and passion much like my father's. Paul says that what he most values from his lifetime's engagement with fishing are "the spiritual returns and the getting there."

Getting there has been a means, not an end, for Paul, and it has for me, too, though I believed for years that it was not only an end but the whole point. Now I think back to the porky rainbows in Lake Alice near the top of Mount Kenya, and to the Labrador brook trout in their spawning colors; I think back to float-fishing the Jardine River in northern Australia, with its crocodiles and baby tarpon and saratoga, and to other float trips on the Beaverhead, the Missouri, the Penobscot and Nolichucky, the Mulchatna, the Gol Gol and Motueka and Tongariro; I think back to the elegant houseboat fishing for big browns on Chile's Lago Yelcho, and to the choppy sea off Bahía Pez Vela with droves of sailfish riding every wave; to the twenty-five-pound jack salmon that ate a skated bomber one morning with Chris Child and Vicky Mills on the Miramichi, and the four bonefish over eight pounds in two hours with Big Glenn at More's Island; I think back to fishing for wahoo with black pearl diver Jean Tapu off the South Pacific island of Apataki, and for bluegills in an Iowa farm pond with Ralph Ellison; to catching snapper in the surf of New Zealand's Ninety Mile Beach, and dorado on flies with Buby Calvo in northern Argentina; to dapping live mayflies for brown trout in Lough Corrib, and throwing Chernobyl ants to giant pike on Minipi Lake, and nymphing for piranas in the marsh behind Los Ombucs; I think back to the jungle rivers on the east coast of Costa Rica, to the Great Barrier Reef, to the lakes of Tasmania and the Northwest Territories—and it seems to me now that those places and experiences were not at all destinations, as I had believed them to be—a series of valleys stretching farther and farther away into the horizon—but more like waystops on a round journey that has brought me back to within walking distance of where I started.

For a couple of years before my father's death in 1988, he and I fished together often again at Lake Tadpole. His kidneys were failing and he would sleep on the drives to and from the lake, but he was wide awake and as thrilled as always during the two or three hours we were there. I ran the electric motor and fished him in the bow, as he used to fish me. He still whooped every time he hooked a fish and cackled as he played it, his self-assured face as soft now as a Bahamian sunset and split as wide as ever with the joy he took in that place. Though I was closing in on fifty years old by then, he would still bark at me to get my worm in the water whenever it was not, and to fish in my half of the boat. There was still plenty of lake for both of us.

Now I live back in Birmingham for six months each year. Lake Tadpole belongs to me. I built a boathouse out there this past spring, on the same concrete pilings that supported the old one that burned, along with my father's cabin, in the seventies. And next year Patricia and I are going to build a cabin of our own on the west shore of the lake and live in it while we are in Alabama.

Lake Tadpole is the water I find myself fishing most often now, both in fact and in my dreams, and for the first time I am trying to really *learn* how to fish it. A few weeks ago I bought an electronic fish finder, not so much to find fish with as to learn the bottom and the structure of the lake, and I realized that ever since I was thirteen years old I had fished at this place, my home water, only superficially and insincerely—as I have fished at many of the waystops—and that now I have the time to know it.

No more than five miles down the road from Tadpole, tacked to the wall of a ramshackle barbecue joint owned by a fiercely cheerful, three-hundred-pound black man named

Woody, is an article about Woody's great-aunt Eunice, who is 104 and still loves fishing more than anything else in life. There is a picture of Aunt Eunice sitting on the shore of some pond in her lawn chair, undemonstratively fishing with a long cane pole. Beside her chair is a minnow bucket, which the article says she still carries herself, along with the chair and the pole, down to whatever water she is fishing for the day. Aunt Eunice is quoted as saying, "I don't know why, but I'd rather pull 'em in even than eat 'em. I reckon I've always been that way."

I plan to invite Aunt Eunice out to Lake Tadpole before she turns 105, and let her set up shop on the dock and teach me something about minnow fishing. Judging from her face in the picture, she will find the time to do that. Judging from the picture and the write-up, Aunt Eunice *owns* time—to get less done; to go nowhere but a nearby lake or river whenever she can find someone to tote her; to know things rather than do them: time like prayer; connective time.

Ted Hughes, the late poet laureate of England, was a fervid salmon fisher. When asked shortly before his death how he accounted for his lifelong passion for fishing, he mentioned "the fascination of flowing water and living things coming up out of it—to grab at you and be grabbed." Then he said, "Oh, I think it's an extension, isn't it? It's an extension of your whole organism into the environment that's created you . . . It gives you the opportunity of being totally immersed, turning back into yourself in a good way . . . to the most valuable things in yourself. The unspoiled. That feeling of something absolutely sacred and unspoiled is a big part of that, isn't it?"

I'd love to have Ted Hughes and my father out there too with me and Aunt Eunice on the dock at Lake Tadpole. I've love to have the four of us together one fresh day this April, when the dogwoods are out and the bass and bluegills are on the beds, with not a cloud of bad luck in the sky and time on our hands to whoop and cackle.

◆   ◆   ◆

When I asked my agent and good friend, Dan Green, what he thought the introduction to this book ought to cover, he said, "Well, it *has* to answer one question, Charles."

"And what would that be?" I said.

"Why a grown and reasonably intelligent man would waste as much of his life as you have on fishing. What else?"

The truth is I don't know why. But I do know some of the things that fishing has given me in compensation for my time, wasted or not. It has given me the names of rivers I can say to call up images that calm and steady me. It has taken me on countless occasions, and continues to, into the sweet, welcoming trance of instinct and back to the sacred and unspoiled parts of myself. It has given me a kinetic, engaged, and vivid life that in my natural dreaminess and laziness I probably would not have had without it, and connections to the surfaces and sounds and smells of waters and woods, of boats and ropes and tents, of marshes and flats, of daybreak and deep night and mountains and campfires, of birds and fish and the holy, open ocean—of many of the animating mysteries of this world. It has given me a way to find both pride and humility. And it has given a big part of my life a progress, a growth and forcing through, a rendering; it has allowed me to catch and to be caught, to leave and to return.

Granted, all of that may not justify the years I've spent with a worm in the water, Dan. But then again, it may.

Bon Temps with
Rebel in a
Sportsman's
Paradise

WE PULLED INTO THE PARKING LOT OF PREJEAN'S
Restaurant in Lafayette, Louisiana, a little after noon on
December 2—three dusty, road-hardened anglers with appetites.
We had not had a single unforgettable meal since dinner sixteen
long hours before, and we were understandably impatient for our
next one. This was, after all, the heart of Cajun country, where
even the alley cats eat brilliantly. Moreover, Tom and I had
learned long ago that you cannot bring all you have to this sapping
business of fishing and dancing and eating and drinking your way
across an entire state without regular sustenance of a high order.

We meant business, Tom Montgomery, Jody Bright, and I.
Our plan was to get in and out of this lunch, prepared especially for us by one of the best Creole chefs in Louisiana, as
quickly as possible—thirty minutes, max—and on into the
Atchafalaya swamp, where we faced twenty-four grueling hours
of birdwatching, bass fishing, and more great eating. On this
ninth day of a thirteen-day angling road trip, Montgomery and
I had already fished for redfish in two locations, labored

through a Cajun Thanksgiving where the good food was knee-high, grazed the oyster bars of Abbeville, and stuffed ourselves with fried alligator while dancing the Cajun two-step at Randol's here in Lafayette. There was more hard work coming up: more redfishing after the Atchafalaya, and at least one night of eating and partying in New Orleans. This was Jody's first road trip. He had joined Tom and me only four days before, and we were having to teach him a little about pacing. As we entered the restaurant, I reminded him gently that this was just a job like any other job. All we had to do was keep our eyes on the ball.

We were there at Prejean's to meet Jody's mother's old friend Becky Stokes and Becky's secretary, son, and boyfriend, and a person named Rebel Kelley. Becky had been helping us organize our trip. Rebel Kelley, assistant director of the Louisiana chapter of the Coastal Conservation Association, was coming down from Baton Rouge to fill us in on the redfish conservation work of that valuable organization. And for our dining pleasure, Becky had asked her friend James Graham, the esteemed executive chef at Prejean's and also at his own Fish and Game Grill in Lafayette, a man who has been called in print "the most innovative master of wild game cookery in America," to demonstrate those very skills in a special presentation—on which the others were already waiting at the table when we arrived.

We greeted Becky, her boyfriend, her son, and her secretary. Staring at a delicious young blond woman on the other side of the table whom I took to be the son's wife, I asked Becky, "Where is the guy from the CCA?"

"I'm Rebel Kelley," said the blonde.

"You're not."

"Rebel *Anne* Kelley, really." She grinned up at me, and my old heart just flopped right over.

I met the late poet and novelist James Dickey at an academic party one night in Wisconsin when I was in my early twenties and he in his late thirties. We got drunk together on red whiskey, appalled a professor or two, and then lay down on somebody's living room floor and arm-wrestled. I beat him, whereupon he grabbed my head joyfully in both his big hands and whooped, "You're one of *mine*, god*dammit!* Boy, you're one of my *own!*"

Periodically throughout my life, maybe once or twice a decade, I meet a woman who instantly makes me want to shout the same thing; I see in a female face a particular shining mingling of beauty, wit, and unabashed appetites, and I just want to pop a straw in that person and drink her. This cannot properly be called a crush. I am a very happily married man, and I get pretty much the same feeling every time I look at my daughter, Greta, and at my seventy-two-year-old quail-hunting friend Peggy Pepper. I just happen to have a strong affinity for lovely, unafraid women with a sweet tooth for life. And here, in Prejean's Restaurant, was clearly such a woman.

Over the next two hours or so we drank a few bottles of wine and we ate: shrimp wrapped in applewood-smoked bacon, pepper jack cheese, and grilled tasso, then deep-fried; a pheasant, quail, and andouille sausage gumbo that won the state gumbo championship six years in a row; fire-roasted yellowfin tuna; south Texas blackbuck antelope with black butter crawfish; and Acadian bread pudding with coconut, caramel, and pecan sauce. Rebel Kelley had a Cupid's-bow mouth painted with ardorous red lipstick, smart, inquisitive eyes, a sense of humor, and an unhidden disdain for regulations. She was thirty-two years old, the age of one of my sons. "We educate and legislate" is all I can remember of what she told me, professionally and at length, about the Coastal Conservation Association. My own professionalism, case-hardened as it usually is on these trips, was already weakened by the wine and the sublime food when Rebel finished it off completely over dessert.

"You know, my two favorite things in the world," she said, "are fly-fishing and cocktail dresses."

I didn't grab her head and cry, "You are one of my own!" but I might as well have. "Come with us, Rebel Anne," I said, sealing my fate and that of my co-road-trippers. "Come with us into the Atchafalaya!"

"Okay," she said, "but I have to go get my fly rod first."

"Hey, Chuck," said Jody, when we were back in our rented white Pathfinder with all of his coolers tied messily on top. "I'm still learning the ropes here, so I need you to fill me in on something."

"Anything, my boy. Just ask."

"What kinda ball is it exactly we gonna be keepin' our eye on out there in the swamp with Rebel?"

◆　　◆　　◆

Well, the thing is, you have to be light on your feet in this road-tripping business, as *well* as beautifully organized. You have to leave yourself open to a certain amount of serendipity. You can't afford to be afraid to paddle onto a good wave when it comes along, whether you're exactly ready for it or not. It would have taken too long to explain all these principles to Jody, so I just decided to let the road be its own hard tutor, as it had to Tom and me.

"Sportsman's Paradise" is what the state of Louisiana calls itself on its license plates. Being sportsmen chronically in search of paradise, Montgomery and I had taken that, the very moment we learned about it, as a personal challenge to mount one of our patented sorties of sporting exploration, camaraderie, self-indulgence, mishap, passion, and revelation. We had made similar trips to Montana and Florida, two of a number of states that might legitimately advertise themselves on their license tags as sportsman's paradises; but it was only Louisiana that had done so. The boldness of that appealed to us—who as road-trippers had learned to value boldness over all—and we determined to put the claim to a fair test.

We began this trip, as we had our previous one to Florida, in the company of Jimbo Meador. A native of Point Clear, Alabama, Jimbo is my generation's true Natty Bumppo, the dead-center real thing in a world suddenly full of outdoors knockoffs, who throws a cast net as well as a fly line, who studies birds as lovingly and skillfully as he hunts them.

"You know why white pelicans have those black feathers on the ends of their wings?" he asked me on the first morning of the trip.

We were in a custom-built Go-Devil mud skiff with guide Mark Brockhoeft, afloat in a marshy estuarial basin of the Gulf of Mexico near Myrtle Grove, Louisiana. This basin is less than a forty-five-minute drive from the French Quarter of New Orleans, but it might as well have been a two-day drive from any civilization for all the sign of it there. There was not a building, nor a road, nor another boat or angler in sight, though it was a clear, calm, inviting day with a climbing temperature in the fifties. We were stopped for lunch, gunwale to gunwale with the skiff holding Tom and Bubby Rodriguez, who, along with Mark, operates Big Red Guides and Outfitters. Mild winter sunlight lay over everything like a blessing. We drifted, eating subs, talking, and watching birds. In the air and on the water were thousands of birds: ibises, herons, egrets, gadwalls, widgeons, teal, and white pelicans . . .

"No," I said. "Why?"

"'Cause black feathers have more melanin. They're stronger.

The pelicans need the strength down there to get their lift." Jimbo is out of that line of Southern boys who kept the Civil War going so long by their riding and shooting and skill in the woods, but mostly by the things they noticed that other people didn't. "Nature's really got things figured out," he said, knowing that to be true, and satisfied and consoled as he has been all his life by that knowledge. He grinned at the gentle noon. "She dudn' miss a trick."

We spent the afternoon as we had the morning, poling through clear, shallow water among islands of golden coontail and widgeon grass, looking for redfish to throw flies to. And finding them. Owing to recent, stunningly successful Gulf Coast conservation efforts, redfish are now present from Texas to Florida in good-old-days numbers. The marshes, bayous, and flats that constitute the coastline of Louisiana have become the nation's largest fishery and a gigantic nursery for redfish, fattening them on blue crabs, shrimp, and baitfish until they are large enough (at twelve to fifteen pounds) to move offshore. That nursery is a fly-fisher's playground. At almost any time of year, except during the coldest snaps, Mark and Bubby can put a fly rodder on redfish averaging six to eight pounds—waking, finning, tailing, even "crawling" after food in water so shallow their whole backs are out of it—so many of them that forty to fifty "shots," or casts to individual, sighted fish, is considered an average day.

We drifted and caught fish and watched the clouds of ducks trading the bright, empty marsh. And that first day's mellow, easy abundance seemed a good omen, a promise of largesse to come. The next morning Jimbo went home and Tom and I studied the merry world of New Orleans' Jackson Square for a while over beignets, fresh orange juice and café au lait at the Café du Monde. Then we walked over to Central Grocery and picked up for our lunch two of the great, greasy meat and olive salad sandwiches known as mufulettas, and drove our Pathfinder west through Baton Rouge and into Cajun country.

Traveling west on I-10, you enter that country as if through a looking-glass around the town of Henderson. Suddenly all the men seem to be wearing camo. There are hand-lettered signs advertising catfish and gaspereaux, lots of dead dogs and nutria along the roads, alligator-skin stores, raised cemeteries, little roadside crosses commemorating fatal crashes, dual Rottweilers in a few front yards, and bass boats and jet boats in the others. A billboard near Crowley showed us Bubba Oustelet, "Car Dealer of the Year." A bumper sticker on a camo-painted monster truck said "Coonass and Proud."

"Coonass" is a self-embraced nickname for Cajuns. It derives from *cunaso*, a Carib Indian word (via Spanish), meaning a man who lives simply on and with the land. "Simply" here distinctly does not mean joylessly or witlessly. "Youda *man*, Bubba," I shouted at the giant billboard showing Mr. Oustelet's joyful, shrewd, land-loving face. "These are my *people*," I gushed to Tom.

What I meant was that I loved the Cajuns. I wish I had been born Cajun. For those of you who somehow are not aware of who or what the Cajuns are, they are descendants of (and their name an abbreviation for) the Acadians. The Acadians were among the first white people to settle North America, coming from France in 1604 to settle what is now Nova Scotia. In 1755 most of them were gathered up and thrown out of Nova Scotia by the Brits, and many of those refugees wound up in south Louisiana, where their descendants today number over 700,000 strong and happy souls.

For six months a year I live in Nova Scotia, in an Acadian village settled by escapees and returnees from the 1755 Expulsion. The names there, as in Louisiana, are Thibodeaux and Boudreau and Pettipas. There are boats and Rottweilers in the front yards, faces are more often than not shrewd and fun-loving, and life is lived close to the land. Driving into south Louisiana feels to me like coming home, and I love the same things about the people there (a wondrous anomaly of a people in this job-whipped, pleasure-averse nation) as I do about my Acadian neighbors—their music and hospitality, their irony and devotion to family, their gaiety, and how relentlessly, how wholeheartedly, they *carpe* every single *diem*.

It was on Highway 14 from Gueydan through Abbeville and New Iberia and then on 90 East through Franklin and Morgan City that I began my Cajun music appreciation initiative for Tom's benefit. I stopped at a Wal-Mart and surprised him with Wayne Toups, Waylon Thibodeaux, Bayou Pon Pon, Raisin and Almonds, the Cajun Playboys, Nathan and the Zydeco Cha Chas, Beau Jacques and the Zydeco Hi-Rollers, and Fernest Arceneaux. With shrewd, joyful, land-loving music pouring out the windows of the Pathfinder, we sped past cane-fields, some of them burning, ricefields, and oil wells.

Then we were in Houma, where everyone seemed to have a Ram 1500 truck with an ATV in the back; where we could have driven into a Mitsubishi dealership and gotten a picture taken of ourselves with Santa. We were there to fish with a redfish guide named Danny Ayo, but that was not until the following day. To fill up that afternoon, Danny had mentioned on the phone that his wife's brother-in-law, a shrimper, might take us out on his boat.

Vincent Menge, his wife, Anna, and his seven-year-old son, Opie, lived in Chauvin, south of Houma, in the middle of Bayou country. They greeted us when we arrived in their drive-way, blasting Cajun music, as if they had been hoping for months we would come. Vincent was short and stocky, with brushy black hair, dark skin, lively and friendly hazel eyes, and the most purely delighted face I have seen in years. He and Opie took us out for a couple of hours on their twenty-nine-foot shrimp trawler, the *Captain Opie*.

Vincent was forty-one, one-hundred-percent Cajun with a one-hundred-percent Cajun life. That morning he had shot a limit of ducks in an hour and a half before breakfast. He was carefully teaching Opie to hunt, and the week before the boy had killed two teal with one shot. Vincent shrimps for six months and does carpentry work for the rest of the year. He has been a shrimper since he was fifteen, and for years he ran a sixty-two-foot open-water trawler until he got tired of the overhead and being away from Anna and Opie so much. Now all his shrimping is done inshore, and that leaves more time for the rest of his life. When the shrimp run out in late November or early December, he shoots ducks, geese, and deer, and traps nutria, mink, muskrat, and otter until the end of February. Then, until mid-April, he and Anna crab. Pretty much year-round Vincent fishes—for bass, specks, and reds inshore, and for bull reds, cobia, and tuna in the Gulf. Last year in December and January alone he caught eighty-six speckled trout between two and a half and six pounds in the Bayou right off the boat dock forty feet behind his house.

"The good Lord's been kind to me. I'm a very, very, very happy man, bru," he said. He was grinning, setting out his winglike trawling nets on either side of the boat and stating an evident fact. Opie ran around helping him. The scrappy, homemade-looking little *Captain Opie* chugged down the bayou toward the Gulf. "If you get bored or unhappy living here, man, there's something *wrong* with you. And Anna does it all with me. Shrimping, everything. Best thing ever happened to me is my wife. You know, we've been married eighteen years and I don't leave the *house* without her, bru."

Shrimping is best at night. Night after night during the season, Vincent and Anna and Opie go out at dusk, set their nets to the white light of moon and stars, and come in again just after dawn. All we caught in the nets that afternoon were a few jellyfish, and on the way in Opie talked to his dad about different kinds of jellyfish and what they can do to you. Though the white shrimp season had three more weeks to run, Vincent thought they had already gone, moved back into the deep water of the Gulf. He had had a pretty good season, grossing close to $28,000. In order to net twenty from that, he does his own engine work, builds his own nets, welds his own A-frames and skimmers. He earns another ten thousand dollars or so from his carpentry. Thirty, thirty-five thousand a year is all he and Anna and Opie need to be happier than kings. "My old man told me a long time ago it's not what you make, it's what you save. We have everything we want, bru, and money in the bank." How could this be, you might wonder, as I did: "We make our living off the land as much as we can. We eat what we catch and trap and shoot. We don't buy much."

I asked Vincent about the legendary Cajun disregard of fish and game limitations. He grinned; it's a question Cajuns have learned how to answer. A man who fishes and hunts to feed his family, Vincent said, becomes a conservationist by necessity. It's the corporate boys who are in it for the big profit rather than subsistence who do the real damage, like the huge, steel-hulled, V-12 open Gulf trawlers he called "slabs" that are putting the white shrimp in decline by overfishing and fishing inshore—working lakes and bayous, sometimes in water as shallow as three and a half or four feet when they draw five, tearing up the bottom and muddying the water.

It was almost dark when we tied up back at Vincent's pier. Anna was waiting for us. The next day was Thanksgiving, and she and Vincent invited Tom and me to eat Thanksgiving dinner with their family after we finished fishing with Danny. "We have plenty of food, bru," said Vincent. "No end of food."

He and Anna stood in the driveway with an arm around each other, their faces radiant in the closing dark. I opened the driver's door on the Pathfinder and asked Anna what they had in their life that kept them so happy. I told her I would put whatever it was in this story and maybe it would help somebody. "Us," she said after a pause, hugging Vincent and motioning to Opie. "Just us together."

Danny Ayo, who is married to Anna's sister, laughed the next morning when I told him what Vincent had said about Cajun conservation. "Even coonasses learn. Listen, we used to measure the fish we caught in *boxes*. Same with ducks. But that way of doing things carried to extremes is what led to gill-netting out the bayous, and the purse-seining in the Gulf that took all the breeding-stock redfish. When there weren't any redfish around anymore is when the Cajun got to be conservationist. But now that they're back, we're taking *care* of them. Like I say, even a coonass'll learn."

It was early on a calm, cool, flawless Thanksgiving morning and we had just run from a boat launch to the mouth of the first bay we were going to fish, somewhere in the enormous system of marshes and bayous that extends for over thirty miles south of Houma to the Gulf. We could hear the guns of duck hunters around us, but, as at Myrtle Grove, there was not another angler in sight, though this place, too, was literally crawling with redfish. I had just stood up on the casting platform in the bow of Danny's skiff and was stripping out line, with the fly lying dead in the water twenty feet away, when a thirteen-pound redfish ate it. After we released it, Danny poled into the bay and redfish scattered like rats off the shallow bottom ahead of us, leaving trails of mud boils.

The pug-nosed, blue-collar, toe-to-toe fighting redfish can go from piggishly indiscriminate to confoundingly picky in his eating habits day to day, and sometimes even hour to hour. Occasionally, one will munch any old fly dumped right on his head, or even his tail, or four feet away from him. More often they can be even spookier than most bonefish and the *only* productive cast drops the fly two feet in front of a cruiser and a foot beyond him so that it can be retrieved virtually into the fish's mouth. Even then sometimes a red won't eat it, particularly when the water and the air are cold, as they were that morning.

I caught a few fish; we ran over some; a few more wouldn't eat. Then Tom took the push pole and Danny Ayo took the casting platform with his Orvis 1-weight fly rod. When asked why he prefers to use a fly rod designed for quarter-pound bream while fishing for six-to-twenty-pound redfish, Danny answers, "Why be normal?" But there is also the fact that he would like to break the current thirteen-pound, three-ounce world record for redfish on two-pound tippet, and he believes the 1-weight is the rod God wants him to catch that fish on. A while back he boated an eighteen-pounder on two-pound test and let it go because it was not caught on the 1-weight.

Usually he fishes alone when he is not guiding—a thin, intense, opinionated man, born-again, casting the tiny little rod from the poling platform with the pole gripped between his knees. He enjoys solitude—"When I work by myself, I get along with everybody," he says—and he enjoys difficulty. He built his house himself. He built his eccentric one-off boat and trailer himself, learning how to weld from a book. He is a photographer, a carver of decoys, a maker of stained glass, a truck-driver for Consolidated Freight, and a redfish guide, when he wants to be, on Saturdays, Sundays, and Thursdays.

Danny devoutly worked a few fish with no appetites: "That's the *one*, that's the cast . . . God *wants* me to have this fish!" After one of the reds gave us the fin and swam off in a huff, Tom, on the pole, said, "I'm afraid in my apostasy I'm not helping you."

Then Danny caught a six-pounder, very nicely on his 1-weight. Then I caught one, an eight-pound tailer. Then Tom hooked a monster of maybe eighteen pounds and his leader broke at a knot . . . The fish had turned on a little bit and there were thousands of them. In a lifetime of redfishing I have never seen so many reds in one area, and Danny Ayo and his clients have them all to themselves.

Ducks were flying, and ibises and terns and pelicans. We pushed up a flock of roseate spoonbills and watched them ignited by the new sun. The sky was a speckless blue dome, and under it we worked and caught about a dozen fish, having the pure fun that even impure men can have at fishing. Then at eleven-thirty we ran back in for Thanksgiving dinner.

Danny's wife was there, and Anna, as well as Sonny and Rosabelle Arcenaux's other two daughters and one son and all the children and spouses, all crammed into Sonny and Rosabelle's little house across the highway from the Menge's. Sonny and Rosabelle's kids live within ten miles of that house, and they and their children and spouses were so intimate with each other, so welded together by daily familiarity, that, like my Nova Scotia neighbors the DeCostes, they seemed to be connected parts of the same organism rather than separate individuals.

The twenty-plus relatives and one poodle welcomed Tom and me in among them as if we were old friends suddenly returned home, with something different, richer and more comforting than hospitality—something more like passing the big platter of their intimacy and pleasure in each other around for us to share as we did their food.

As for the food, there was gumbo, turkey, a roast from a deer that Vincent had killed, pork, turnip greens, macaroni and cheese, potato salad, fried French bread, pies, and cakes. There was also cold beer and football on the tube, and the young cousins playing games in the front yard, and everyone laughing at Sonny's jokes. He and Rosabelle had lived in this two-bedroom house since they were married. The four daughters had grown up sharing the extra bedroom. The son had slept in the washroom.

"Do you know what the Cajun motto is?" one of the daughters asked me when she brought me a piece of pecan pie. She was smiling. She had wonderfully calm and affectionate eyes.

"*'Laissez les bon temps rouler,'* and you Arcenaux really know how to do it."

"There's another one," she said, "for other kinds of times. *'Lâchez pas la patate'*—'don't let go of the potato,' it means. Hold on; keep going. We know how to do that, too."

The next day we drove back to New Orleans to pick up Jody Bright at the airport, then headed west again after tying his two big coolers on the top of the Pathfinder. Jody was planning to fish with us for a few days and then go on to south Texas, where he grew up, for some deer and bird hunting with family and friends. He had packed his clothes and a duffel bag in the coolers. As all the ducks and deer and redfish and quail and what-all that he had promised to folks back home in Kona, Hawaii, went into the coolers, the clothes would come out and go into the duffel. The plan left us looking like a bunch of Okies with a beer habit, but that (and most everything else you can think of) would never bother Bright.

Abbeville is a charming town where you could easily eat

yourself to death. Before soldiering on to more fishing, Tom, Jody, and I took a couple of lay days there staying a few miles outside of town at a camp on the Vermilion River graciously provided to us by Jody's mother's old friend Becky Stokes. The spunky Miss Becky fairly fizzes with optimistic energy. The oil-related company that she owns and runs with her sons was turning a wonderful profit. She had a good-looking boyfriend named John who once managed the king of Malaysia's holding company, and a brand-new purple Jag with a license plate that read EZ2ENJOY. She looked as though she had never been bored a day in her life; as though she would chew up and spit out boredom.

Her camp on the river had a bass pond and a bonfire pit, tame geese and ducks, and a comfortable old house with a tin roof built on the site of a pre–Civil War sugar cane plantation. Using it as a base, we drove around the live-oak, lime-green ricefield country of cattle and egrets, crawfish ponds, sugar cane, and bayous. We visited an alligator farm with Becky and John, we caught some bass in the pond at the camp, and we ate. Abbeville may be more serious about good food than any other town its size in the United States. Even the local Texaco station advertises shrimp stew on a sign underneath its gas prices. At Shuck's, Dupuis, the Riverfront, and Black's, we ate shrimp, oysters, gumbo, frog legs, crawfish, catfish, and alligator. Then Becky suggested we get serious about our Cajun chow and go up to Lafayette with her and John for a meal and a *fais-do-do* at Randol's.

A *fais-do-do* is a Cajun dance; they have them every weekend at Randol's, and, believe me, you have not done that until you've done it.

We met Becky's Cajun friends Virginia and Dayton there, and all of us sat at a table on the edge of the big dance floor

drinking pitchers of beer and eating fried crawfish tails, alligator bits, and boiled crawfish from a platter stacked a foot high
with the delectable little mud bugs.

Out on the dance floor were thirty or forty couples doing
the Cajun two-step, the Cajun waltz, and the Cajun jig to the
impossibly lively music of a band called Filé, and having so
much pure, stark, unfettered fun at it that the thought crossed
my mind when we first sat down that maybe there was something not quite right about them. Moving counterclockwise as
they danced, with expressions on their faces as if they had all
just learned they were getting huge raises for working fewer
hours, were old folks and kids, snappy young hotshots with
bandannas on their heads, full-figured guys in John Deere caps,
a popular seventy-seven-year-old gent named Leopold who
looked under fifty and never missed a dance, and a little dark-
haired bouncing girl whose face was completely transported by
the music.

"There's everyone from gas-station attendants to doctors
out there," said Virginia. "Hairdressers, lady lawyers. Cajun
dancing's a great equalizer." Women were asking men to dance,
boys asking fine women, old men asking girls. "Aren't you guys
going to ever dance?" a woman asked Tom and me.

"We're watching," I told her.

"We don't understand watching," she said. "We would just
flat wither up."

After a while I did dance a two-step for fun with Virginia to
a tune called "Matilda," then a waltz, then a jig. And I wanted to
never leave the floor! I wanted to learn how to yell *Ayouuuuu!*
the way the Cajuns do.

The next day we put our game faces on and went back to
work. We were headed for the Atchafalaya swamp, then on to

more redfish flats near Slidell, but first our job demanded that we have lunch at a place in Lafayette called Prejean's with Becky and John, Becky's son and secretary, and some guy from the Coastal Conservation Association named Rebel Kelley.

◆   ◆   ◆

Rebel met us at the Butte La Rose landing on the Atchafalaya River with her fly rod and a rainsuit. The sky was bruised and stormy, but she looked up for anything, as bracing and blond as a bank of daffodils in the fog.

"You travel light," I said. "Most women would have at least two suitcases for a night in the swamp."

"What do you mean, 'a night in the swamp'?"

"We're spending the night. Didn't I tell you that? In a cabin."

"Get *out*," said Rebel. "I don't even have a toothbrush."

"You can use mine," Jody said, with south Texas charm.

"Are you guys kidding? Coerte, are they kidding?" she asked Coerte Voorhies. He shook his no-nonsense, military head. Rebel shrugged. "Well, what the hell—we'll see how it shakes out. I just hope somebody brought some red wine."

"We gotcha covered there," Jody told her.

Coerte had driven Jody, Tom, and me out from Lafayette after our lunch at Prejean's to the landing, where his son, Kim, was waiting with a boat. Coerte and his wife operate a bed-and-breakfast in an 1820 plantation house in Lafayette, and Coerte and Kim run a swamp tour business called The Atchafalaya Experience. Coerte is sixty-seven, a burly, energetic, well-spoken ex–military man and small-arms instructor who still wears a camo uniform every day and carries a 9-mm automatic on his hip. His family has been in this part of Louisiana for two hundred years. His grandfather lived to hunt and fish, he told me; so did his father; so do his son and grandson. And him? "Are you kidding?" he said. "What else is there? And we live in the best place in the world for it. This is a sportsman's paradise."

Kim Voorhies, who looked to be in his early thirties, had a *bon temps* face. Retired from the military with a bad back, he also wore a camo uniform, causing Tom to wonder if there might be some kind of survivalist action going on back there in the swamp. I don't think so. I think the Voorhies' outfits are part of the way they represent their product—a way of announcing that when you leave the landing at Butte La Rose with them and head downriver, you are heading into serious Tarzan country.

Between its defining levees, the Atchafalaya Basin is seventeen miles wide and sixty miles long—860,000 acres of swamps, lakes, bayous, and water prairies. It is the largest and the last of the great river-basin swamps in North America—a stuffed mastodon representing a particular vanished form of American wildness. Over three hundred species of birds—including more than fifty thousand egrets, ibises, and herons, and the largest nesting population of bald eagles in the south central United States—are found in the basin. Sixty-six species of reptiles and amphibians live there, along with red wolves, black bears, cougars, bobcats, deer, possums, otters, nutrias, minks, and coons. And over ninety species of fish and shellfish make it one of the richest fisheries in North America, one in which the fish take alone can average one thousand pounds an acre—two and a half times more than the Everglades; more than in any other natural water system in the United States.

For almost two centuries Cajuns lived in the basin in cabins and on houseboats, using floating grocery stores for what little provender they couldn't take from hunting and fishing and trapping, from crabbing and trotlining and crawfishing and hoop-netting. Now, by law, they live outside the levees, but they can keep cabins in the basin, and boats. Some still make a living there; and many more, like Rennie and Barry Serrette, who live and work in towns, would tell you they still *do* their real living there.

As soon as she walked into their camp and introduced herself, Rennie and Barry recognized Rebel from her appearance a few months before on the cover of *Louisiana Sportsman*. It was a cover they remembered well, as it pictured a couple of their major enthusiasms at once: Rebel had been wearing a bikini and holding a fish. Rennie and Barry were very happy, if a bit surprised, to see her dropped mysteriously—like that Coca-Cola bottle in *The Gods Must Be Crazy*—into their camp in the swamp, and were happy, too, with Kim and Tom and Jody and me for providing her. Rennie mentioned that they had had very few beautiful young sportswomen stop in on them lately.

The Serrettes' camp was just upriver from the Voorhies' camp; it was bigger, with a few more amenities, so Coerte and Kim had arranged for us to take our meals there. After a rained-out fishing and birdwatching trip across the river to Cow Island Lake, we went back there for dinner bearing good red wine, a bottle of George Dickel, and a few Upmann cigars, all of which were almost as well received by the brothers as Rebel had been.

Barry was a carpenter and Rennie—an engaging and soulful man—a pharmacist in Baton Rouge. They were the first generation in their old Cajun family not to live in the basin and make a living there. But they both spent every day they could at their family camp, and their times there—living as simply as their ancestors had—were their best times. They fed us alligator sauce picante and Cajun navy beans with jalapeños, cooked on a woodstove, and nothing we ate in New Orleans was any better. Afterwards we drank Dickel and smoked, and talked about being Cajun.

"It's not ancestry, it's an attitude," said Rennie. "A Cajun gives you everything he has. He never holds back. Drink hard, sleep hard, cook hard, hurt hard."

And apropos of how central cooking is to Cajun culture, Barry, who had cooked our meal, made the following gnomic comment: "You know, really, the only difference between hot and cold Cajun food is the temperature."

Back in the little Voorhies cabin, Tom went to sleep, Kim cut up some venison for breakfast in the morning, and Jody and Rebel and I lay in our bunk beds considering conservation. Rebel had borrowed not only Jody's toothbrush but his sweatpants to sleep in, and he promised her, with more south Texas charm, that he would never wash them. The great swamp was soughing outside in the black night; Pink Floyd was playing on the boom box; and the music mixing with the moist swamp air felt weirdly liberating and expanding.

Rebel said that though the Louisiana CCA had had good success in the past few years with many of its efforts, the state's coastal marshes—which comprise a full 40 percent of the nation's coastal marshlands—were being lost at the terrifying rate of more than 25,000 acres, or fifty square miles, a year. Those acres were being lost to the erosion that results from the dredging of more and more oil-access and shipping canals, and by the decrease in delta plain sedimentation caused by channelizing the Mississippi. Unless something was done to turn that loss around, Rebel said, it would not be too long before it was all over but the shouting for the kind of inshore fishing we had been enjoying. Then they could just change the license tag.

Lying in her lower bunk in Jody's sweatpants, Rebel talked

with heart and good sense about Louisiana conservation, and it made me happy to know she would have a hand in the future of it. Because I wanted to hear more about it from her, and not at all because of her general luster and verve, I felt disinclined to quit Rebel's company when we left the Atchafalaya. So the next day—after we had breakfasted on venison, Cajun sausage, and eggs, and after a second boat ride among the creased cypress stumps of Cow Island Lake, during which she plied her fly rod quite nicely in a difficult wind but caught nothing—I said, "Why don't you meet us over in Slidell tonight? We have a house this time, with a shower and a toilet and everything. You can go fishing with us and Jimbo and Paul and Gary tomorrow, and maybe one of us will hook a fish for you and let you reel it in." That is Alabama charm.

We were back at the Butte La Rose landing, and Coerte was there with our Pathfinder.

"Get *out*," said Rebel.

"Why not?"

"Okay," she said. She had to spend the evening with her boyfriend, Charlie, in New Orleans, but she would meet us in Slidell the next morning before we went out fishing. There are two things you learn about Rebel after very little time in her company: she is not an amateur at life, and she is a woman who will never be down for long.

"Good job, Chuck," said Jody when we were headed east. "I sorta thought we needed to keep our eye on the ball a little longer, too."

◆　　　◆　　　◆

On the drive down to Slidell, Tom and Jody and I—for lack of anything better to do and inspired perhaps by the raunchy music of Nathan and the Zydeco Cha Chas—invented a character named Buck Boudreau, who, despite our best efforts to control him, kept gesturing rudely and shouting salacious things in a faux French accent to pretty young Cajun misses as we flew past them.

Not really.

Really what we did was talk about fishing, like the simpletons we are. When we had all thoroughly tired of the ear-exhausting Cajun music, I turned on NPR, hoping for some soothing Liszt or something. What we got was Purcell's opera on King Arthur. I turned up the volume, hoping to upgrade my young friend Bright's musical taste. I drove and from time to time helped Sir-somebody conduct. Sitting in the passenger seat, Jody listened disinterestedly for a while, then with growing animosity.

"That can't be the same Purcell who played in Willie Nelson's band," he said witheringly at one point. "Ned Purcell?"

"Hush," I told him, "and listen to this sublime plethora of horns."

"Would you *please* turn that shit *off?*" he asked a little while later.

"Not right now. We're coming up to Guinevere's magnificent aria."

"Uh-huh. Yeah," Jody said after a moment, and looked out the window. "That's always been one of my favorite parts, too."

Just before we arrived at Gary Taylor's house, he said, "Hey, Chuck, is a plethora something like a nutria?"

"Not really," said Tom. "I think it's a little bigger."

Gary Taylor is a wiry, enduro-motorcycle-racing fishing guide. For seven years he was a tournament bass fisherman. For the past nine he has owned and operated "Go For It Charters" out of Slidell, a town forty minutes northeast of New Orleans, just off of Lake Pontchartrain near the Mississippi border. His wife, Vicki, an entomologist with a sensible Louisiana specialty in mosquitoes, met Tom and Jody and me at her door and told us "the best fisherman in the South" was down in the garage.

He was checking over the sixteen-foot Hewes Bonefisher skiff and one of the twenty-two-foot cats that we'd be going out in the next day. With him was Jimbo Meador, who had driven back from Alabama to join us on this last leg of the trip.

Gary had arranged for all of us to stay at a friend's weekend house on a bayou outside of town, and after we rigged some plans for the following morning and for dinner that night, he led us over there. Parked in the driveway—as unmistakable as Elvis's gold Cadillac—was Paul Bruun's van.

Bald, bearish, sensitive, and courtly—a veteran like Jimbo and Tom of my sporting and spiritual quest in Florida a year and a half before—Bruun is the sort of uniquely inspiring example to road-trippers everywhere that Jimi Hendrix was to guitarists. He is a trout guide, writer, sports fan, and raconteur extraordinaire from Jackson Hole, Wyoming, and one of the best all-around anglers alive. He is also one of the most catholic and curious, tracking down new fly patterns for snook and spinnerbait techniques for bigmouths with equal alacrity.

Every year in November and December, Bruun leaves Wyoming for a nomadic and idiosyncratic month or longer of sport, country-music appreciation, and gourmandizing. He drives first to Texas for bass fishing, quail hunting, and duck and dove shooting, staying all around the state with various friends. Next he goes to Louisiana for more bass, redfish, speckled trout, and ducks; then on to Florida, his native state, for the angling smorgasbord down there; to Alabama for the smallmouth fishing in Pickwick Lake; and finally to Nashville for the Grand Old Opry. On the way back home, he stops off for a day or two at Cabela's sporting goods store to do his Christmas shopping. All along this route, Bruun chases down food, music, and fishing leads: buying hams in an Alabama country store he read about somewhere, and tasso, andouille, and hot sauces throughout Louisiana; visiting somebody in Tennessee to learn about a "revolutionary jighead system with a straight worm"; pilgrimaging to the Meridian, Mississippi, home of Jimmy Rogers, the Singing Brakeman.

In his home on wheels are a half-dozen dress shirts on hangers, shotguns and shells, three sets of boots, hip boots, a couple of pairs of waders, a dozen baitcasting, spinning, and fly rods with two or three reels and extra spools for each, and close to ten thousand lures and flies. It is the van of a passionate and tireless bloodhound, who chases down and brings to earth along the highways of America what he calls "the inner game" of the things he cares about.

Paul was upstairs in the borrowed house, sorting through his tackle. After welcomes and a few beers, we all went to dinner with Gary and Vicki at the Indian Village Catfish Restaurant and pool hall, where David Allen Coe was singing on the jukebox and a shy, seafood-loving chihuahua ran around eating what few scraps of catfish, alligator, and shrimp anyone would spare him.

We left from a boat landing at dawn the next morning, and Rebel was there to meet us, exactly on time and ready to *rouler*. We made up an imposing fish posse: Gary with his Hewes skiff and two big-engine, shallow-draft cats, Jimbo with a fourteen-and-a-half-foot Wilderness Systems kayak that he likes to fish from, Rebel, Tom, Jody, Paul Bruun, and me, and three friends of Gary's—Ralph Smith, Jim Lamarque, and Dave Hall, the legendary Louisiana game warden.

The Louisiana, or Biloxi, Marsh—which Gary Taylor has almost as much to himself as Mark Brockhoeft and Danny Ayo have theirs—is a vast offshore system of grass islands, creeks, and ponds. Another forty-five miles or so offshore are the Chandeleur Islands, which Gary also day-fishes with his fast cats. In combination, the two areas give him and his clients a twelve-month fishery for redfish and speckled trout, shark, ladyfish, blue runner, mackerel, snapper, wahoo, and even a few largemouth bass in the marsh.

We didn't catch any bass that morning, after a choppy twelve-mile run across Lake Borgne to the marsh, nor did we catch many redfish, as the cold, windy weather had them "sulled up." Around midmorning a cloud bank moved in, making it even colder, so we pulled all three boats up to a houseboat that Gary uses in the marsh and had on it an early lunch and some storytelling. When we went fishing again, the sun was back out and the fish hungrier. After kayaking for a while with her fly rod, Rebel got in one of the cats with Jim and Dave and Jody, and fielded those boys all afternoon like a major-league shortstop. They also got serious about putting some speckled trout in Jody's coolers, keeping twenty-two out of forty they caught. The redfishing picked up, too. Bruun caught more of them than anyone else, playing his inner game with a variety of arcane plug-rod techniques.

And Jody got to show off his road-trip-improved vocabulary. Late in the afternoon, he and I and one of Gary's guides were poling a little pond, casting to occasionally finning redfish. A nutria swam by.

"There goes a nutria," said the guide.

"Naw, his back's too big," said Bright. "That's gotta be a plethora."

After a considering pause the guide said, "Maybe. But we haven't seen many of them out here lately. The commercial trappers like to got 'em all."

We ate our penultimate road-trip dinner at Gary's house that night. Vicki made the best gumbo we had yet eaten on the trip, out of chicken, oysters, and andouille sausage, and it preceded a wonderful Greek vegetable casserole and redfish fillets cooked skin and scales down on the grill. With more than a little wine, Gary and Vicki, Rebel, Jim, Paul, Jimbo, Tom, Jody, and I toasted the meal, the fine day, the trip we were finishing, and the paid-off promise for it of richness and plenty that I had felt on the first day.

I hugged Rebel as she was leaving to drive back to New Orleans and told her I would miss her. I told her she had sort of been to our trip what one of those carved female heads was to the bow of a nineteenth-century whaling ship, and the comment seemed to make some sense at the time.

"Y'all are not through with me yet," she said. "You and Tom and Paul are *mine* tomorrow night when you're in New Orleans. You know I told you about my two favorite things? Well, I left one out."

Could I be hearing this right? I wondered. Was it the wine? Did Tom and Paul have to be in on it? I tried to smile casually. "Get *out*," I said.

"Y'all have been taking care of me in the swamp and all, now I'm going to take care of you. Charlie has to work, so I'm going to take y'all to dinner and then we're going *dancing*."

The next morning, after telling Jimbo and Gary good-bye, I dropped Jody and his coolers off at the New Orleans airport, wishing him well with all his new words in south Texas and congratulating him on his good work habits throughout the trip. Then I drove on in to the Hotel Monteleone. Tom and Paul were exploring around Slidell and were coming in later.

I had a dozen oysters, a catfish po' boy, and a couple of Abita beers at the Acme Oyster House, then walked down Julia Street to look at some art. Later I took a workout on the top floor of the hotel and then a rest, and after that I felt ready for pretty much any way Rebel could come up with to take care of Tom and Paul and me.

At eight o'clock we all met in the hotel lobby and walked over to the C&E Courtyard Grill. Paul was dressed like an English squire, in a tweed cap and jacket; Tom and I were in old fishing clothes two weeks from a last washing; and Rebel was dressed all in black, simply to kill. We had a good Creole-meets-Asian meal at the C&E, a meal you'd rave about anywhere but in New Orleans and anytime but at the end of a thirteen-day eating binge. Then, around ten-thirty, we turned ourselves over to Rebel.

Driving her white Explorer with dispatch, she took us uptown—an area, she said, that the serious partiers prefer to the Quarter—up St. Charles past the Camelia Grill to a bar and dance-floor joint called The Maple Leaf, where Rockin' Dopsie Jr. and the Zydeco Twisters were playing.

Rockin' Dopsie Jr. was a stringy black guy wearing a black cowboy hat, an apron, and a metal washboard called a *frottoir* on his chest, who could strictly make music. Zydeco is jukin' Cajun, Cajun soul music, Cajun dirty-dancing—a beat rather than a melody, and Rockin' Dopsie Jr. and his band owned it. The dance floor was chockablock with bodies shaking and clapping and twisting and shouting and high-five-pointing, and every face had a grin on it. Rebel was the queen of the place. She tore it up—dancing up on the bandstand with Dopsie, pulling me and Tom up every time we tried to sit down and dancing with us both, clapping and pointing at the ceiling and whooping "Ain't life fun, or *what?*" her yellow head bobbing like a beacon.

We danced until the place closed at two. Then we got back in Rebel's Explorer and she whipped it down the weekend uptown streets, past all the dowager, decorated-for-Christmas mansions on St. Charles, through stop signs and over curbs, anywhere she wanted to be, finally pulling up on somebody's yard to park in front of the F&M Patio Bar—where things were just getting going and the crowd looked like the mother of all frat parties.

We danced there, too, on another floor so crowded with *bon temps rouler*ers that some of them had taken to dancing on the pool table, including a girl in a silver dress with a heartbreakingly beautiful waist-hip relationship who swayed and clapped between the rails, her eyes closed.

Rebel introduced me to the F&M's owner, Trevor, who also owned a fishing lodge in Belize and had a face like a choirboy with no conscience. Later she and I found ourselves at the bar eating cups of red Jell-O marinated in 151-proof rum while she told me, with her hard, clear, bright good spirits, about an imperfect childhood. I told her about meeting Jim Dickey. Then I took her face between my hands, kissed that child on her forehead, and broke the news to her that she was now one of my own.

We finally said good-bye to Rebel in the Hotel Monteleone parking lot just after four-thirty, two and a half hours before my plane left. She backed away down the street, waving and blowing kisses, and I stood watching her, realizing that she would have walked on coals that night to show the three geezers in her charge a good time, and that maybe she had; that in her untiring gaiety and readiness for anything, her generosity and inattention to the regs, in her death grip on the *patate*, Rebel belonged on the cover of *Louisiana Sportsman*'s every issue, as the state's poster girl. If Tom and I and our various hearties had learned anything about Louisiana after two weeks and 1,600 miles, it was that the place goes for broke whether it has a toothbrush or not. And if that's not a working definition of a sportsman's paradise, I don't know what is.

HOOKING

MR. WILL

IF YOU ARE A PASSIONATE ANGLER, THE CHANCES ARE THAT someone caused you to be that by hooking you on fishing when you were young. Those of us who are hooked young, by someone who knows what he (or she) is doing, rarely get off, and often we turn into fishers of kids ourselves.

My father set the hook on me before I was six by taking me out with his friend Captain Otto Hahn, on Otto's old commercial fishing boat, to fish for redfish around the jetties off Mayport, Florida. By the time I was eight, my dad had graduated me to fly-fishing for bream and bass in Alabama lakes, and I have skewed my life with fishing ever since. I have also jumped at every opportunity to skew other young lives along the same lines, beginning with my own three children, all of whom could fish before they could ride a bicycle. Now, with those children grown and no grandchildren yet, I have to rely on friends who married later in life than I did to keep me in fresh prospects.

My friends Hayes and Patricia Noel from California have a great kid named Willy. When Willy was six years old he said to me, "Charles, when I turn ten I want you to take me on a fishing trip. And I'd like for you to put some real thought into where we're going to go." (Honestly, he said something very close to this; Willy is also a bright and mouthy kid.) The next year Willy reminded me that there were only three years left before our fishing trip. The following year he reminded me twice that we'd be ripping lips in only twenty-four months. And when he was nine, he said, "So. Where are we going to go next year, big guy?"

"Someplace good," I told him. "I'm putting some real thought into it." And I was. The cardinal rule to hooking kids on fishing is simplicity itself: make sure they catch plenty of fish. I wanted a place where Willy could do that; also one where the fishing would be easy and fun and the tackle requirements uncomplicated. And finally, I wanted a place palpable enough to burr up for a lifetime in his memory, as Otto Hahn's boat had in mine.

I had recently learned about the amazing bass fishing in Mexico's Lake El Salto, where, I was told, it was almost impossible not to catch a lot of fish; where you had thousands of acres of textbook bass cover virtually to yourself, and some true footballs swimming around in that cover; where you stayed in a comfortable lodge in palpable Mexican countryside, enjoyed excellent food, and fished from good boats with Mexican guides. I decided this would be just the ticket for Mr. Will, and he agreed. I also decided to invite his father, Hayes, and my younger son, Shelby, to join us on the trip.

Shelby was gut-hooked on fishing by a sailfish twenty years ago when he was five, and he has never spit the hook. Hayes, on the other hand, has never felt one: he remains one of those mysterious people who are content to regard fishing unheatedly, as an occasional pastime. As much as I love him, I have never tried to salvage Hayes from this condition. I have never even so much as made a cast in his direction, believing him to be too old and stubborn to bite. But I was also determined that Hayes's twisted disinterest in fishing would not be passed along to his only son and one of my favorite people on earth. In short, I had a high-stakes job to do in Mexico. Having Shelby along, I figured, would be a big help. Hayes's presence would only make the challenge more interesting.

I missed a connection in Boston and arrived at Billy Chapman Jr.'s Angler's Inn on Lake El Salto eighteen hours after Shelby, Willy, and Hayes. They had come in the night before, fished that morning, and were taking an after-lunch siesta when I arrived, driven up for two hours north from the west coast city of Mazatlán by Tony Encinas, the lodge's general manager. A smiling young man named José, the assistant manager, met my arrival with a big frozen margarita, and on his heels came a sleepy-faced but excited Willy who hugged me and, being rarely at a loss for words, told me nonstop over the next fifteen minutes all about the fish he had caught that morning. I regretted not having seen those first fish caught and, in their catching, Mr. Will himself open his mouth to take the bait. But in less than an hour we were all out on the water again, Willy and I in one boat and Hayes and Shelby in another.

Situated picturesquely in the foothills of the Sierra Madre and sprawling in the shape of a cartoon moose over 17,000 acres at low water to 25,000 acres during the rainy season, Lake El Salto was created in 1986 by damming the Elota River. The impoundment was established by the Mexican government to provide irrigation for the opening up of new farmland, but Billy Chapman Sr., a top fishing and shooting outfitter in Mexico since 1966, and his son saw other potential for it. Along with the government, the Chapmans stocked the river with Florida-strain largemouth bass in 1985, and during the next rainy season those bass introduced themselves into the new lake, finding there a bass El Dorado. With all kinds of freshly flooded structure for cover, no predators, and an enormous food supply (in the form of shad stocked by the Chapmans, and tilapia stocked by the government to establish a commercial fishery in the lake), the El Salto bass have flourished like Samoans, growing at a rate of up to two pounds a year.

Just coming into its prime, El Salto regularly produces catches of one hundred and even two hundred bass a day per boat. Most of those fish are in the one-to-two-pound class, but there are plenty of hogs as well. To wit: the lake record is twelve pounds three ounces; last year Billy Chapman found a sixteen-pound bass that had died from choking on a two-pound tilapia; and the week before we arrived, two anglers with a film crew caught ten bass around ten pounds apiece on a *single morning* on "jigs 'n' pigs," and even got it all on film.

Those are the kind of to-wits that can build expectations in young and grizzled alike, and I was as fresh on the bit as Willy as we sped up the lake in one of the lodge's tricked-out Super-17 Trackers, piloted by a guide of few words (and those in Spanish) named Xavier. The steep and ragged Sierra Madre reared all around the lake; the empty countryside was tan and dusty, and the water of the lake a milky, fishy green. We shut down in one of the lake's northern coves and drifted into a line of flooded trees. Xavier let down the electric motor and sat on the head of the Yamaha outboard to run it. Willy and I were in business.

He took the bow and started to cast. Two months before, while I was on a trip to California, we had gotten him and his father geared up with spinning outfits. Willy's was a six-and-a-half-foot glass Fenwick rod and an open-faced Shimano reel loaded with fifteen-pound mono. On that same trip I had taught Willy how to cast, strike, and play a simulated fish and tie a clinch knot, and he had been practicing those things at home. Now he had a tackle box full of lodge-recommended lures—Zara Spooks, Rattletraps, Woodchoppers, rubber worms, and Power Grubs—that he could tie on himself and knew how to cast surprisingly well. I leaned back on a gunwale and watched Mr. Will work the cover like a miniature Roland Martin, his eyes glittering, talking a mile a minute. On the fifth cast, a bass jumped all over his silver Zara Spook and Willy reared back on him. The bass shivered out of the water, then ran for cover. "Keep your tip up," was all I had to say: Willy beat him like a drum. Xavier released the fish, a fat two-pounder. "You can't do better than that," I told him.

"Thanks, man," said Willy with a neon grin.

Willy started fishing around four o'clock that afternoon. By five he had caught four or five small fish and lost a few others and was on top of his game—not missing a cast and working the big topwater lure appetizingly. We had talked about how bass see and hear, what range of water temperature they like and where they find those temperatures at different times of day, and what all that stuff has to do with where and how you fish. I told Willy that at dusk, in the last hour or so of light, bass pick up a visual advantage over much of their food and keep it until dark, and that in that magic Twilight Zone is often where the best and most memorable fishing happens.

I had just finished saying this when Willy and I slipped into one of those zones ourselves. The light went to steel on the water, the sky went orange, the little breeze that had been up went down, and the fishing went wild. In about an hour, Willy —on the first afternoon of his first fishing trip—caught a three-and-a-half-pound bass, lost one over seven, caught one over six and another around five, and caught or lost four or five smaller fish. Somewhere in there I got tired of being a spectator. I strung up an 8-weight fly rod, tied on one of Ron

Kruger's phenomenal Desperate Diver bugs, and caught ten or so bass myself, including one of around seven pounds that was hooked in the gills and bleeding badly. I put the fish in the live well instead of releasing it as we had the others, and it banged around in there for a while until Willy asked me please to kill it. I did that, and Willy mourned the fish. "It's all right," I told him. "There are a lot of bass in this lake."

After a minute Willy said, "That's like saying it's all right to kill someone because there are a lot of people in the world."

"Who's teaching who here?" I asked him.

José met us at the lodge door again with frozen margaritas. After one or two of those with platters of quesadillas that José brought to our rooms, we showered and then ate bass cooked in tinfoil. During dessert, José brought into the dining room a carefully wrapped little box and presented it to Willy. When Willy opened it, a green chameleon lizard popped out and darted down the table and into a crack in the floor as if it had played this gig before. After dinner we sat outside on a covered patio in the warm, bug-clicking night, Hayes and I smoking cigars and drinking Carta Blancas, and all of us telling jokes and stories. Swinging himself in a hammock, Willy delightedly held up his end, and it was as much fun watching him study this fine and subtle part of going fishing as watching him learn to cast.

Hayes and Shelby had caught plenty of fish, too, and Hayes had caught one over six pounds. Shelby was still glowing from their afternoon. I asked Hayes if he had enjoyed himself. "I don't know," he said, this red-hot stocks-and-bonds trader. "Is the fishing good yet?"

Someone suggested that the four of us form a club that would take a fishing trip a year. "Other kinds of trips, too," said Hayes. "Like to topless Club Med resorts," said Shelby. "No . . . but kayaking, maybe," said Mr. Will. I suggested we call this club the El Salto Angling and Adventure Club. But Willy put some real thought into it, and came up with a better name. Then all the members of the Happy Campers' Sporting Club went to bed.

We were up at four the next morning and out on the lake by five-fifteen. Shelby and I fished together that morning, as we have countless times since he was five, and Willy was with his dad. We had a cloudy red sunrise on the lake with a low barometer, and the fishing was slow. Shelby and I threw popping bugs and Desperate Divers into some of the world's bassiest-looking cover and caught about a dozen small fish by seven. Then Shelby hooked, played perfectly, and released a real hog—a bass that brought all the Happy Campers up to at least one fish apiece of around seven pounds. It was his biggest bass ever, and Shelby knows how rare fish like that are. His hands shook a little when he held it up before releasing it, then he hooked the red and white frog popper in the hook-keep, stretched out grinning along the gunwale, and had a long look at the day. I thought about how much fishing it takes before you start to learn the best and untellable things, like giving the other man the boat after you catch a good fish.

We went back into the lodge around eleven-thirty to lunch and to nap until three. That afternoon Willy fished in the boat with Shelby, who introduced him to fly-fishing, and he caught a few bass on a popper. Hayes and I caught maybe forty fish— in between enjoying each other strenuously, as has been our way for twenty years—and he was *still* not sure the fishing was any good. He told me that he and Willy had gotten on each other's nerves a little that morning. I condescended to tell him that was because he didn't know the conventions; nor, I added, did he have much of a generous tutorial spirit. As it happened, I condescended too soon.

"I *love* fly-fishing," Willy told me when we met back at the boat dock at dark, and then he told me that twenty times more on the two-mile drive back to the lodge. He offered to buy the rod that I had lent him to learn on—a 9-weight Winston.

"You can't afford it, Mr. Will," I said. "Besides, it's too big for you."

"No, it's not—I cast it really well. You'll see tomorrow."

We had to leave the Angler's Inn after lunch the next day to get back to Mazatlán. Willy and I shared a boat that morning, and both the weather and the fishing were a little off. All Willy wanted to do was fly-fish and, though it was remarkable how adept he'd become at it in one afternoon, I spent most of the early morning tying and retying leaders, getting wind knots out of tippets, and dodging his errant back-casts. Willy would have the casting rhythm down for a while, then lose it. "Quit whipping the rod, Willy—let the line straighten out behind you," I said more than a few times. With him in the bow, my own fly-fishing range was limited, but for some reason I kept at it, if testily. "Front of the boat, Will. Remember, we talked about how when you're in the bow you cast to the *front* of the boat so the other guy has somewhere to fish? Remember?"

Had I gotten rusty at this or *what*, I wondered.

Around eight, we ran up to the mouth of the Elota River, where there were acres of purple water hyacinth and steep cliffs on either side of us, and a two-foot-long gray and yellow lizard sleeping on a rock. The fishing was cramped and snaggy, and Willy was getting hung up a lot. I finally put my rod up to attend to him full-time. This is what you *came* here for, I reminded myself.

After a while Willy's casting smoothed out, and when a nice bass swirled on some bait in the shallows, he covered the fish quickly and accurately and caught it on a chartreuse popper.

"You're *right!*" Willy said to me. "I let the bug sit that time before I popped it."

"Good going, Mr. Will. You've got it under control now, buddy," I told him.

And he did—or part of it, anyway. I thought of all the other parts he had to look forward to, now that he was good and hooked. I remembered my older son Latham's first big brook trout, caught in a beaver pond in Maine; my daughter Greta's first fly-rod bonefish, caught in Venezuela. I remembered all three of them learning how to short-stroke yellowfin tuna on a boat in the Gulf of Mexico, learning to double-haul, and to paddle a canoe. All that was out in front of Willy if he wanted it to be, along with his first tarpon, tying his first fly, casting into big wind. A lifetime of things.

On the evening of our first day at El Salto, when Willy and I were in the zone—the sun was setting, the bass were on the bite, and the magic of fishing was happening to him for the first time—he said, "I think I want to be a full-time fisherperson like you, Charles." That's neat, I thought. I didn't bother going into the sacrifice in income. It was almost dark and Xavier was getting antsy, but Willy kept on casting. I opened a beer and stretched out, watching him, and thought, in the beer-ad cliché, it doesn't get much better than this. I watched him and hoped very specifically that, full-time or not, Willy would come to love and practice fishing enough that he would have it when he needed it—so that he could call up moments like this one to be his friends when things were desperate or miserable for him. I thought of all the healing and peace and camaraderie that fishing had given me since Otto Hahn's boat, and how memories and dreams of fishing had always been friends I could count on when I needed them. While Willy kept casting into the dark, I drank my beer and hoped hard for another young life to be skewed like that by fishing.

Mr. Will caught a second bass on the chartreuse popper at the mouth of the river and then he sat down. "You can fish now, Charles," he said. "Maybe you've learned something."

ON THE ROAD AGAIN IN GODZONE

NEW ZEALAND IS THE MOST OPTIMISTIC PLACE IN THE world. Today, for example, is already tomorrow in New Zealand, and you can't get any more optimistic than that. Residents of the lovely fruit- and wine-producing region of Hawkes Bay on the east coast of the North Island advertise themselves as being the first people on earth to see the sun rise each day, and I plan to be there with them on January 1, 2000, to witness—a day before the rest of you—the most optimistic single moment of the next thousand years: sunrise on the first day of a millennium as yet unblemished for even a second by human screw-ups.

I myself will almost certainly be beset by grave doubts, and I want to be standing there with a glass of Hawkes Bay Cabernet in hand hard by my man Geoff Thomas when that first millennial sun bulges out of the Pacific. "So how do you think this next one will go?" I'll ask Thomas.

"Ahh, she'll be right, mate. She'll be right."

"You sure?"

"Yehyehyeh," the Possum will say, and, tiring of his poncey little wineglass, will just start drinking straight from the bottle. "*Shitch*yeh."

❖ ❖ ❖

Among the many human enterprises that run rough without the lubricant of optimism, hunting deer from a tiny helicopter ranks right up there with trout fishing—which might be part of the reason why New Zealand is the world's capital for both.

Geoff Thomas's mate Steve "Golfie" Gamble is a legendary commercial hunter of deer from tiny helicopters who got his nickname from coming up with the improbable practice of stunning deer for live capture by firing golf balls at them from a specially bored rifle. A short, quick, wiry man, hard and merry, with a tidy mustache, a tough, boxer's face, outsized hands, and ropy forearms often covered with deer blood, Golfie makes a living by piloting his little two-seater Robinson at treetop level across mountainsides and into the beech-choked valleys of New Zealand's South Island, zigging and zagging behind sprinting deer through country so remote and rugged that walkouts are measured in days, while his son Greg hangs by a seatbelt out the doorless passenger side, either shooting buckshot at the animals or "live-trapping" by firing an eight-foot-diameter net over them from a net-gun at a range of twenty-five yards or less. As well it should, this employment pays well (Golfie and his son gross up to $350,000 N.Z. a year supplying a strong foreign market for venison, antlers, and hides, and a domestic one for live deer), but both the overhead and the risks are horrendous. Nearly sixty deer-hunting chopper pilots and shooters have died on the job since the late 1970s.

Despite its hazards, Golfie relishes his work. He also relishes his downtime, a good bit of which is given over to blue cod fishing, and Geoff Thomas, Tom Montgomery, my thirty-two-year-old son Latham, and I had driven down to the southernmost end of the South Island to join him for a spot of that before working our way north again in pursuit of New Zealand's more heralded trout.

This was near the beginning of the eighth angling road trip Thomas and I have taken together in his country, but the first in nine years of mixed fortunes for both of us. If I had harbored any doubts about whether or not I was still resilient enough for one of his nonstop, balls-out sporting tours, I had lost them over the past two days crawling around in the mud behind the Possum hunting Canada geese near Fiordland National Park, and I was now simply and purely delighted to be under way again in the place where I have always been able to see more clearly than anywhere else on earth the difference between the hawk of living and the handsaw of getting by.

Over the years Thomas and I have learned that it always pays to begin a fishing trip in New Zealand with a confidence booster, a little easy and profligate ripping of lips, before getting down to the often maddeningly real thing with the trout, and Golfie had promised that the obliging blue cod would give us exactly that opportunity. But anyone can just learn something to be true and then act intelligently on that knowledge; Geoffrey and I have always disdained the easy way. When we arrived in Tuatapere, Golfie's hometown, at around noon on the day before the blue cod trip, Tom made plans to go up in the Robinson with Golfie for a tour of the coast, Latham opted for a walk around town, and Geoffrey and I decided to go look for some trout to savage.

Tuatapere calls itself "the sausage capital of New Zealand," but the local restaurant had only one sausage. We split it four ways for lunch, then Geoff and I drove forty minutes north to a little river running out of Lake Monowai that promised to be easy and confidence-boosting, but lied. All afternoon and into the evening we were beaten and insulted by trout that were as obnoxiously picky about what they would and wouldn't eat as

New York models. In fact, as I pointed out to Thomas, for all we caught, we might as well have spent the afternoon casting little cheeseburger flies onto a fashion show runway.

But the next day, drained of confidence as we were, we managed to exact a bloody revenge. After most of a bottle of Scotch and a four-Maalox feed at Golfie's house that night of crayfish tails, mutton chops, and goose and duck stroganoff, no one felt much like rising at 5:30 A.M. to go deep-sea fishing—least of all Golfie and Geoff, who had stayed up yarning and finishing the Scotch for hours after everyone else went to bed. Yet Thomas—at his toughest as usual when the going gets tough—managed to rouse himself into an almost offensive cheeriness by the time we had driven thirty miles along the coast to Gardiner's Bay, a foggy, rocky, desolate sort of place that was our boat-launch for cod fishing.

"Right," he said, rubbing his hands together and bobbing his head as we stepped out of the vehicles into a cold fog. "*Now* we're on a bloody fishing trip, eh, Golfie?"

"Now we're bloody *fishing*," Golfie agreed.

"The point here, mates," said Thomas, "is to catch all the blue cod in New Zealand."

"To catch the *last* bloody blue cod in New Zealand," said Golfie, struggling for emphasis through a terminal-looking hangover.

Geoff and Latham went with Golfie and his son Greg in Golfie's little inboard. Tom and I were in a well-used eighteen-foot outboard with Golfie's friend Horace the bushman and his crew—John, with the beard and long hair and no inclination to talk, and Taylor the Maori. Both boats puttered out together for about a mile through a swelly sea into Foveaux Strait, with Antarctica the next stop south, and anchored up where Horace felt was right, in seventy-five feet of water. Just visible through a lifting fog off our starboard bow was Stewart Island, New Zealand's third and smallest island—the anchor of Maui.

The creation of New Zealand, according to Maori legend, is, fittingly, a fish story. One day the demigod Maui, who lived in Hawaiki, the original Polynesian homeland of the native Maori people of New Zealand, went out fishing with his brothers. They went a long way out to sea—somewhere close to where we were angling for blue cod, in fact—before Maui pulled out his magic fishhook, made from the jawbone of his sorceress grandmother, and threw it over. Soon he hooked a giant fish, so big he had to toss out his anchor to keep the canoe from being towed. That anchor became Stewart Island. The fish he finally wrestled to the surface became the North Island. And the South Island, its entire length lying just off our stern, is what became of Maui's canoe.

The islands were named *Aoteraroa*, "land of the long white cloud," by the Polynesian explorers who discovered them, sailing from Hawaiki (possibly one of the islands in the Marquesas group) in canoes over a thousand years ago, guided only by the stars and a gifted navigator named Kupe. Lying halfway between the Equator and the South Pole, the temperate islands they found—the largest by far in the Pacific—were a virtual paradise: with no mammals other than bats, but with fish-crowded coastal waters and forests teeming with more than 150 different species of birds, including the flightless and luckless moa, which stood as high as ten feet and was soon hunted into extinction for its flesh and feathers by the original New Zealanders. Today, though the moa is gone and the country is not without conservation and environmental problems, New Zealand (or "Godzone," as it is known in and out of the country to the countless numbers of people who, like myself, believe it to be just that) is still like a Noah's Ark of the world's natural pleasures and thrills and beauties and fruitfulness—so completely the other side of the rainbow for anyone who fishes or hunts or otherwise adventures outdoors, that it is still possible there to want to catch the last blue cod.

For two or three hours we gave it our best shot. Using old boat rods with taped-on guides, rusty star-drag reels with arbors one-fifth full of frayed monofilament, two links of a logging chain for sinkers, and big, dull hooks baited with chunks of very ripe cod from the last trip, we began almost immediately to haul up fish. They were greenish blue, long-finned, big-mouthed creatures, about two to five pounds apiece. We also caught some little red, surprised-looking soldierfish. Everything went flopping into the fish box regardless of size or make. Then Taylor brought up a small dogfish shark. With his knife he sliced it up the gills, ripped open its stomach, and cut off its tail before throwing it back into the sea.

"Not fond of dogfish, huh?" I asked him.

"Oh, I got nothin' particular against 'em," said Taylor.

We were catching a cod about every thirty seconds on our boat, and Latham and Greg were doing about the same on theirs, anchored forty yards away from us, while Geoff and Golfie lay on the deck not feeling altogether tip-top. More dogfish met the same fate as the first, and pretty soon our deck was awash in shark blood. The fish box was filling. Mollyhawks, mutton birds, and gulls swarmed around us, picking pieces of shark off the rolling sea. After a while Golfie's puking could be heard over the rock music coming from a tape player on his boat. Our boat was quieter. Though Taylor occasionally hollered while bringing in a particularly good dogfish or cod,

Horace and John fished with somber, wordless intent, their eyes as distracted and hooded as if they were planning a revolution.

On a normal day, Horace told me on the run back in, he and John and Taylor would bring home two-hundred-plus blue cod. I didn't doubt it: we had over forty of the sad-faced, bug-eyed little things in the fish box after only a couple hours of fishing. And how often did they go out? I wondered. As often as they could—maybe three or four times a week.

It was the full-unrestricted-utilization-of-the-resource approach to fishing and hunting—born of plenty, passed along in a gene, perhaps by moa hunters—that is still as fight-provokingly dear to the hearts of many Kiwis as their all-black national rugby team. You used to see more of it all over the country when I first started going there fifteen years ago. Then it was accepted practice to kill many if not most of the large trout you caught; now it no longer is. Then it was common to kill *every* billfish boated in the Bays of Plenty and Islands; now it's not. But your average Kiwi sportsman is still pretty much unmoved by talk of seasons and licenses and limits, etc., which seem to many of them decadent, imported concepts from countries such as our own that have long ago crapped their own nests and now like to natter on about rules and regulations to others who have not yet completed the job. And nowhere is that sportsman more unmoved than in Southland—New Zealand's Wild West. So Tom and Latham and I kept our fastidious opinions to ourselves about how many kept blue cod is too many, and in fact accepted every one that Horace and Golfie offered us for our drive north.

We began that drive about ten-thirty after a cup of tea with Golfie and his wife and four or five of Golfie's friends, two of whom were also helicopter deer hunters. Ten days later in

Auckland we would read about their chopper going down in the bush; miraculously unhurt, they walked out in two days and immediately bought another helicopter. Loaded down with blue cod, abalone, crayfish, and sea urchins from Golfie, we popped in an oldies tape and headed northeast to meet Ron Stewart.

On the drive up, through Ohai and Nightcaps, Mossburn ("deer capital of New Zealand") and Athol—through rolling, grassy ranching country surrounded by distant mountains, where every truck carried two to six herding dogs and every paddock was full of sheep and deer, deer and sheep—Geoff and I gave the young guys the thrill of their lives by singing along with Elvis, Frankie Avalon, Dion and the Belmonts, Dean Martin . . . This was not a sudden inspiration, nor were we unpracticed. Thomas and I have made a habit of singing along in cars laden with good things to eat and drink and headed toward fishing or shooting somewhere in New Zealand, Australia, Montana, New Hampshire, and eastern Canada ever since we met.

That was in 1983. Geoff, who was then as he is now a sort of jack-of-all-trades sporting-media entrepreneur, invited my wife, Patricia, and me over, sight unseen, to appear in two segments of a program he was producing for New Zealand television. We came back the following year to be in a tape he was making for Air New Zealand and the New Zealand Tourist Bureau, and for five years running after that, when he and I were in the travel business together, to scout new fishing and shooting locations. During all those years we sang in practically every car we got into. We also drank our way into song and sometimes sang ourselves drunk on riverbanks, in bush huts, in bars and in restaurants—including the one in the old Marlborough Hotel in Russell, where we closed the place down from sheer heartbreak following our versions of "How Great Thou Art" and the haunting Kiwi national song, "Pokarekareana."

One cannot help but worry about the passage of time, of course—the erosion of prowess and talent and the power to move people. It had been almost a decade since the Possum and I had joined forces on "Heartbreak Hotel," "Earth Angel," and others, and . . .well, you never know. But by the time we pulled into the pub at Garston it was clear from the nearly ecstatic faces of Latham and Tom when they exited the car that the old magic wasn't entirely gone.

We shook hands with Ron Stewart, sixty-five, and his son Geoff, forty, and followed them a few miles down a dirt road to a mountain-ringed meadow through which flowed the storied Mataura River. Near its bank we were served up a refined tail-gate lunch by the Stewarts of homemade bread, pâté, vegetable relish, fruit, and cheese, after which Latham and Tom and I wandered upstream, guided by Ron and his son, for a little refined upstream nymphing in the blue waters of the upper Mataura.

It was so suddenly the absolute other side of the coin from that morning's angling that it was a little dizzying. Like most professional trout-fishing guides in New Zealand these days, Ron and Geoff Stewart are cultivated, charming men— outfitted with American equipment and neoconservationist ethics, and with almost exclusively American clienteles—who would rather drive back and forth over their new Sage rods with a pickup truck than harm a fish. As a neoconservationist American who would love to see New Zealand trout fishing continue to be the best in the world, I find myself aligned with these guys and thanking God for their majority in the country now. But they often put Thomas to sleep. While he napped beside the cars, Latham and I fished for a couple of hours to a few sighted fish, including one of six or seven pounds that I had to go very deep and fine to tempt and finally broke off on the take (without hurting his mouth, I hope). Then we followed Ron Stewart back to his lodge.

Kiwistyle Lodge is located in the town of Glenorchy, population 120, on the northeast shore of giant Lake Wakatipu, forty minutes north of Queenstown. Its setting of young, jagged, and snow-capped mountains bucking out of the lake is so startling it seems like a slap in the face. Kiwistyle holds only four guests, along with photos and fishing books, crystal decanters and mounts and good sporting prints, comfortable furniture, a broad hearth, and a kitchen from which Ron's wife, Ann, turns out consistently memorable meals. But though the lodge is small, the fishery it offers is big and diverse: six premier rivers running into the lake within twenty minutes of the lodge; three spring creeks; three alpine lakes holding brown trout, and river mouths in the big lake; the Mataura; chopper fishing to the west, sea-run brown trout fishing to the south during the whitebait run in December; and camp-out fishing on the Greenstone River.

Unfortunately, virtually all of that was blown out the next morning by a heavy rain that went on all night. But we were able to stalk a little spring creek and spot a plummy cruising brown trout in the turquoise water.

There ought to be a big sign where you first come through customs at the Auckland airport that says, G'DAY AMERICAN TROUT ANGLERS. WELCOME TO THE NFL. In some places and at odd times, trout fishing can be easy in New Zealand; but typically and essentially, it is more technically challenging and butt-kicking difficult there than anywhere else in the world. There are a number of reasons why that is so, but chief among them is that much New Zealand trout fishing and all the best of it is done by what the Kiwis call "stalking." You walk quietly and slowly, well back from the bank of a river, stopping every fifteen seconds or so to study through Polaroid glasses the usually air-clear water for fish holding on lies or feeding. First you must be able to see the fish; then you must see it before it sees you; then you must put a fly in the only place it can be put to drift naturally over the fish without spooking it. One of the many challenges of fishing in this way for the first time in New Zealand is that the trout you find are, almost always, monstrously bigger than any you've ever caught before, and just looking at them can make you forget which end of the rod does the casting.

"That's the biggest trout I've ever seen," said Latham without glee about the spring creek brown. "Why don't you try him, Dad?" Though my elder son has lived in Auckland for over three years and has fly-fished for most of his life, this was his first time stalking New Zealand trout, and the brown simply gave him the willies.

"No, you're up," said Tom, who understandably preferred Latham as a photo model over me whenever he could get him.

Permit me just a bit of bragging here. There were two dozen ways to blow that fish, and Latham didn't exercise any of them. Instead, he made his way up to the bank in a crouch, false-cast across stream out of the fish's vision, then turned the cast and dropped his parachute hopper with a nymph tied beneath it exactly where it needed to be. The trout porpoised languidly and ate *both* flies not two feet from where Thomas and I hunkered in the grass watching. Latham fought the fish neatly and released it. It was a male of around twenty-three inches, and my perennially happy son looked as happy as I have ever seen him when we all shook his hand.

We had another fine picnic lunch after casting Wooly Buggers at the mouth of the Greenstone. We looked at the Route-burn and Dart Rivers, and we drove up the long valley of the braided, bouldery Rees, then got out and walked to a high saddle looking upriver to nine-thousand-foot mountains that surrounded the valley like an amphitheater.

We were standing in a huge, tilted meadow leading up to a steep and gorsey hillside where merino sheep were grazing. The sun was just beginning to emerge and it fell through the clouds onto the valley and across our meadow like a rain of bright arrows. It was a place to make you want to pray, or find new hope, or pledge yourself to something, or break into "The Hills Are Alive . . ."; a place where the frangible pre-ciousness of life blindsides you like a rogue wave. There are motives and motives to fish. For over forty years one of mine has been to see with my own eyes what lay in the next valley over. Blessedly, fishing allows you to believe that every time you throw a hook in the water something outrageous, as big and bright as your hopes, might swim up out of the unknow-able dark and eat it; and traveling to fish allows you to enter-tain the notion that the next valley over might be the ultimate one, the one finally commensurate with your ability to fanta-size it. For fifteen years I have known that if such a last valley over exists, it does so in New Zealand, and now I believe I may have glimpsed it.

◆   ◆   ◆

Dave Hern stopped his Trooper on top of a hill, took his rifle off the backseat, and scoped the valley and forested hills for a deer.

"It's too hot," he said after a while. "The mongrel cunts are all bedded down."

He and I got back in the vehicle and followed the steep,

rutted dirt road down into the valley to his hut on the Mohaka
River. Geoff Thomas, Tom, and Latham pulled in right behind
us in Geoff's Toyota truck. Geoff had flown from Queenstown
to Auckland the day before and driven through most of the
night to Napier to meet up with Tom and Latham and me. In
the back of his truck, under a camper top, he had provisioned
wine and beer, duck breasts and fish from his freezer in Auckland, all kinds of fishing tackle, sleeping bags, waders . . .
enough stuff to get us at least started off right on the North
Island leg of our trip. We had met Hern near Napier and con-
voyed north on a hot, clear, breezy day through the tan hills,
apple orchards, cornfields, and vineyards of Hawkes Bay, then
by dirt road into the foothills of the Kaweka Mountains and
onto the 1,400-acre block on the Mohaka that Dave and a
group of his friends lease for hunting and fishing.

Because the South Island has so much more wild country
than the North, there is a common perception that the North
Island has very little. This perception is as wrong as the one
that has there being exclusively rainbow trout on the North
Island and browns on the South, when in fact world-class fishing for both species exists on both islands. The Mohaka, for
example, is in some of its stretches primarily a brown trout
river; and some of those stretches run through country as
remote and wild as any on the South Island. At Dave Hern's
hut we were eight miles from the nearest upstream road and
fifteen from the nearest one downstream, at the bottom of a
steep valley flanked by pine hills. Out in the "wop-wops," as
they say in Kiwi—in red deer, wild pig, and big-trout country.

Hern is a sometime guide and part-owner of Hamill's Hunting and Fishing Shop in Hastings. An ex-beef-boner and rugby
player, one of the country's best sporting clay shooters and a
top dry-fly angler, he is a big, strong lad of thirty-nine years,

about 250 pounds, and excellent Kiwi humor and energy. We ate cold chicken sitting on little plastic chairs in front of his hut, then wadered up and started stalking the bank a few hundred yards downstream. There were lots of fish, some of them big. There was also a gale-force wind tearing down the gorge directly into our faces, making the fishing—with fifteen-foot leaders, weighted nymphs, and indicators—a pain in the ass, frankly. We all caught a few trout nonetheless. My best and worst was a slabby twenty-one-incher who wouldn't get out in the river and tug. Dave threw a rock at him, loudly calling him a mongrel cunt, but it didn't help: the trout just stayed in a little backwater finning geriatrically and looking up balefully at me until I took the nymph out of his mouth. It is at such times that someone who fishes as much as I do can wonder where his life has gone astray.

But by seven-thirty we were all standing around outside the hut in the windy dark drinking from a jug of Italian red and watching Geoff cook mallard breasts and snapper fillets on the grill, and I had decided she'll be right. The lights of Thomas's truck were trained on the grill, and its tape player was blasting out Chubby Checker, the Beach Boys . . . Geoff was shaking his shallow butt, wearing a head lamp of Tom's, his sneaker laces untied as always, his shirt open and little possum belly spilling out, flipping fillets on the grill. "Mariaa*aaaa*," he crooned along in his good baritone, reaching his arms up to the starry heavens.

While killing the jug after dinner, we learned from Geoffrey —in a passionate argument the details of which I couldn't for the life of me remember the following day—why the biggest threat to New Zealand was the Indonesian Navy.

"The *Indonesian Navy?*" Tom asked him about halfway through his harangue. "I didn't even know they had one."

"Yehyehyeh," said the Possum. "*Shitch*yeh. The second largest navy in the *world*, mate. You see, that's what I mean: the sneaky little bahstads even have you Yanks fooled."

The five of us finally turned in to sleeping bags on double bunks in a back room of the hut that was the size of a service-station bathroom, and despite the threat from the Indonesian Navy I never slept better.

We fished downstream again the next morning in less wind, and Latham was high rod with five good trout. Around eleven we came back to the hut for a brunch of venison tenderloin, eggs, snapper, and wild boar and duck sausage that Geoffrey had stayed behind to cook, then went upstream for two or three hours where the fish were sluggish and unhungry in the low, warm water.

We left the Mohaka that afternoon, spent the night back in the endearing art deco town of Napier, and drove northwest the following day to Turangi on the south end of Lake Taupo, New Zealand's largest lake. On the way, we stopped for a picnic lunch and a two- or three-hour fish with Tony Hayes on the Rangitaiki River. It was a bright, handsome day, with just enough breeze to stir the tall clumps of toi-toi grass. We ate a picnic beside the river, then Latham, Geoff, and I took turns fishing a few pools and I got a chance to catch up with Tony, who owns the Tongariro Lodge in Turangi, one of the best fishing lodges in New Zealand or anywhere else. We talked about a magical afternoon we had spent together on the lower Tongariro, and a day of helicopter fishing on the world's best rainbow river when he and I watched but couldn't bring to the fly the biggest resident rainbow I ever expect to see, a fish that dwarfed the nine-pounder I had just caught.

There is maybe nothing in the angling life as satisfying as

tacking up memorable new experiences with friends with whom you have shared unforgettable old ones. In the first pool we fished on the Rangitaiki, an effusive adolescent girl of a pool, Tony suggested I try a parachute golden stonefly in the riffle at the top. I tied on this odd choice of a fly, threw it up to the head of the riffle, and caught a beautifully proportioned three-pound rainbow that jumped all over the pool. Tony calling the shot like that, and the memory of the fish hanging like a red comma in the blue air, would have made the entire trip to New Zealand for me if I had needed it to.

In Turangi we stayed with Geoff's mate, Bob South, in his comfortable home there. Southie, as he is called in his adopted country, is a fifty-year-old Californian who moved to New Zealand in 1969 to play and coach basketball. He shortly went from that pursuit to sportswriting for the *Auckland Star* newspaper, and for the past five years he has been the editor of *Fish and Game New Zealand*, a magazine that was named the best in New Zealand in 1996.

In the all but monolithically male culture of New Zealand, *keen* is one of the most complimentary adjectives you can use about someone, incorporating as it does much of what is most valued in the Kiwi character. As it is used there, the word's primary meanings are energetic and passionately engaged, but it also says obliquely that someone is rugged, durable, generous, game for anything, and of course, optimistic (which quite often among Kiwis means the same thing as game for anything, as in "Are those sharks man-eaters, you reckon?" "I dunno, mate; let's jump in and find out."). All of my favorite Kiwis are *keen* keen: so keen that being in their company is like carrying around a very sharp knife. And Bob South is as keen as any of them. It is hard to know whether he stayed on in New Zealand because he was already keen, or whether New Zealand made him that way, but either way he is the real thing in spades and even has by now the accent and the inflections to go with it.

Good food and good wine are two things Southie is keen about, and he dined and wined us marvelously while we were his guests. Fishing is another thing, and he arranged some memorable angling for us, including a day for Tom and me and himself in the Whanganui Gorge, into which keenness took us and was barely sufficient to bring us out.

The day before that particular travail, we floated for five hours down the Upper Tongariro River with Garth Oakden, a good young rafting outfitter from Turangi and a friend of Southie's. The legendary Tongariro was one of the greatest trout rivers in the world when Zane Grey began writing about it in the second decade of the century, and it is even better now, with the *average* rainbow caught in it weighing over six pounds. It is also one of the most comely rivers anywhere—wide and majestic in its lower stretches, muscular and plunging in its upper reaches, six miles of which we rafted with Garth, stopping to fish five or six pools from the bank along the way.

Between the pools were some Class III and IV rapids and lots of bouldery chutes, steep drop-offs and places where the current ran directly into sheer, moss-covered rock walls. The river was milky blue from volcanic sediment, and it ran through placid, inviolate country of native beech, moss, and tree ferns— a wonderfully shrouded and prehistoric-looking country, with candied green patches of sunlight lying throughout it like cobwebs. Wood pigeons and shags flew over us. A blue duck bobbed down the rapids just ahead of us, and swallows and fantails buzzed the river for insects. Latham caught a couple of silvery, vividly striped five-to-six-pound rainbows on weighted nymphs, and I lost one that might have been bigger. The fishing was slow because of an overabundance of sediment in the river, but it was as enjoyable a half-day float as I have ever taken. And we could have repeated it the following day after, say, sleeping late; but every road trip seems to require of me that I spend at least one day flailing around at something over my head, and I had not done that yet.

We dined that night at Tongariro Lodge with Bob South and his girlfriend and Peter Church and his wife. Peter is one of the country's elite fishing guides, one of the best fly-rod anglers I know, and unbeatable company on or off a river. And Peter *knows* keen. When he found out Tom and I were planning to go into the Whanganui Gorge with Southie, he grinned at me as I was declining dessert after an enormous meal and said, "If I were you, Charles, I'd stuff it in. I think you may need it tomorrow."

Geoffrey had to return to Auckland for a couple of days and Latham, with impressive presentiment, decided to take the day off—so it was only Tom and I who drove up the next morning with Bob South to a two-thousand-acre Maori-trust sheep station called Whangaipeke, about an hour west of Turangi. There we had a cup of tea with Wayne Tonks, manager of the station, and discussed how we would spend the day. There was, said Wayne, some fifteen kilometers of good, easy-access fishing on the Whanganui both upstream and downstream, but he understood that we, being keen, wanted nothing to do with such fishing but desired to try instead the isolated middle section of the river including the gorge, was that right?

"That's us!" roared Southie, who had wanted to fish the middle section for some time, believing that in its isolation it might harbor some trout bigger than the river's average of two and a half to three pounds. He asked Wayne how long he estimated it would take us to fish down through it, taking our time, and

Wayne said four to five hours. Then I told Wayne that I had a pair of replacement hips and explained that though I had no problem walking all day on fairly level ground, a lot of up and down gave me trouble. It was all pretty flat, he said, easy wading, plenty of crossings. Which taught me later, after I reflected on it, that the deeply keen do not see things as you and I do. Wayne also said it was a wild, rarely fished, and beautiful piece of water we were going into, and he wished he was going with us—that it was like chopper fishing without the chopper.

In a near frenzy of optimism, Bob and Tom and I packed our daypacks with fishing and camera gear, a sandwich, a drink, and a sweater. Then we grabbed our rods and climbed behind Wayne and one of his ranch hands onto two four-wheel-drive ATVs and rode for thirty-five minutes over rough hills to a high, steep bluff overlooking the river.

"Here you are, boys. Good luck," said Wayne. "If you're not out by dark, I'll come upstream looking for you."

It was eleven-thirty by the time we scrambled down a nearly perpendicular bush-clad track to the river. We came out at a pretty place called the Paradise Pool, where Tom immediately caught two trout between three and four pounds apiece, a brown and a rainbow. Convinced now that we had hit the jackpot, we worked downstream, hopping around each other, spotting when we could and fishing blind when we couldn't. It was a perfect, windless day, bright and warm. The high cliffs on either side of the river were covered with an old growth of beech, rimu, and tree ferns that could have played the forest around Adam and Eve's garden. KIWI KEENNESS WINS OUT read the headline: we were in a glorious place having glorious sport on a glorious day. For about an hour and a half—and then we entered the gorge.

I have neither the space nor sufficient stomach for recalling it to do that ordeal justice, but here is a synopsis. The charming little river we had been on narrowed, steepened, and commenced to run as if trying to escape a mugger, convulsing through crooked chutes and around car-sized boulders. Walking in the river was all either up and down those boulders or wading around them in fast water over stones that were as slick as grease-covered bowling balls. The crossings were almost nonexistent. After I fell on a rock and badly dinged my knee, I tried taking to the shoreline, which was, on the bank I was confined to, a precipice of sawgrass, nettles, and thorn bushes that I was happy to clutch frequently, fly rod in mouth, to pull myself along.

As we clambered and stumbled and climbed our way through the gorge, we also fished a bit, though impatiently, since we had no idea how much farther we had to go or how long that going would take. In a pool little bigger than a bathtub, I saw my indicator twitch and set the hook on an honest monster of a rainbow, well over eight pounds, that jumped once within ten feet of me, then powered over the downstream lip of the pool, ran out all the fly line, and broke off, leaving me with both legs wedged between boulders. It wasn't that the fishing was bad that made it disappointing (we released ten or twelve trout between us—most of them porky rainbows with lipstick-red cheek patches and lateral stripes—and lost more), it was that it had to be an afterthought to getting out of the gorge before dark and in one piece.

Which we managed to do, but only. We came out at six-thirty and there was Wayne casting from a rock, waiting on us. Delivered, I started wading to the first flat shoreline I had seen in almost five hours, slipped on a stone, and fell on my favorite trout rod, breaking it emphatically in two.

By the time we reached the vehicles that Wayne had brought

up, it was seven-thirty. Tom and Bob and I had been on the river for eight hours and had spent maybe three of them fishing. Southie was limping on his bad knee. Tom's bad back was sore. My hips felt like they had gravel in them, my knee was swollen, my rod broken. We were cold, wet, and, temporarily at least, all out of keen.

But not Wayne, who said he reckoned there were plenty of Americans who would pay top dollar to do what we did today.

Could be, Tom and I agreed.

Wayne gave us a few beers for the road and a whole roasted leg of mutton. After falling on the sheep back at Southie's house—in good company and with three or four good bottles of wine—and after a soak in the hot tub and a soupçon of port for a nightcap, I went to bed actually feeling grateful for the harrowing, young buck's day—and even more grateful that with Hughie McDowell we'd be very unlikely to have another one like it.

Hughie is an Irishman, well started on his fifties, who loves fishing and life with a poet's ardor, but has been a little put out over the past few years with the latter. When I first met him in '83 and for quite a while after that, he was an enjoyer of strong drink and an untiring teller of jokes and stories, with the bright sun of his bilateral Celtic personality out more often than the moon. He fished and tied flies, as he still does, on a level of his own, and he guided angling clients that he liked on that same level, mostly around his hometown of Rotorua and into the sublime backcountry rivers of the Urewera and Kaimanawa mountain ranges. As we sat one day beside the most beautiful of those rivers, he invited me to have a sup from a silver pocket flask he carried with him everywhere. It had a funny, intimate message engraved on it, signed by "Knuckles," which was what he called his wife and best friend. Five years later, Knuckles was dead, and Hughie was neck-deep in debt and his moon came out and stayed out. He quit smoking and drinking and even guiding for a while, and some of his friends said he wasn't the same old Hughie and disappeared from his life. But he never quit fishing, and it didn't quit him. In fact, it may be what kept him around—arguing with him, bargaining—during some of the worst of his bad times since '89. And now that he's better, with the big hole in him sewn up, fishing goes with him everywhere the way the flask used to—in the car, to restaurants, home—like a calm old physician who did the sewing.

Latham and Tom and I met Hughie at noon at Rainbow Mountain on the road between Taupo and Rotorua and followed him to a tiny spring creek with lime banks of cress and duckweed that ran through a little Shangri-la of a dairy farm that belonged to some friends of his. The owners were blond, shy, happy, handsome people with three blond sons and a picture-book farm, house, and flower garden. From the house we drove down through a fat paddock full of dairy cows to the little creek—as different from the gorge of the day before as any place to fish for trout could be—and I saw immediately why Hughie liked to come here. It was tranquil and cheerful at the same time, the creek flowing daintily between a high, brushy bank that was good for spotting, and it was technical. The water was slow and impeccably clear; casting would be hard from the bank, and you couldn't get in the creek without spooking whatever you were fishing for: the place was a little graduate seminar in trout angling.

And Latham was ready for it, I believed. He had been fishing well throughout the trip, particularly during the last week, and I wanted for him now a trial trout, one he had to sweat over to catch. Hughie spotted it near the upstream end of the creek's fishable water—a good rainbow, finning under some cress near the opposite bank with just his nose sticking out. Latham had already caught an easy, smaller fish and he believed this one would be easy, too, but he had a hard time getting a drag-free float over the trout, and it ignored two or three different nymphs. Hughie and I were watching from the high bank above the creek. We were talking, but Hughie never took his eyes off Latham and he was grinning as he talked. Latham tried casting from farther downstream and then with yet another nymph, and still the fish showed no interest.

Latham looked up at us and shrugged. "I'm going to try a dry," he said.

"I think the fish knows you're there. I don't think he's going to eat," I told him, remembering numerous times in New Zealand when I have overfished a trout, including one spring creek brown on the South Island that Ray Grubb and I put more than twenty different flies over. It never spooked, but I believe now it could have told us what brand of waders we were wearing.

"Try a dry," said Hughie.

"How about a big Royal Wulff? It might make him mad."

Hughie chuckled and said, "Cast your line up here to me. I've got a great bloody ugly fly for you, and if *it* doesn't piss him off, nothing will." He caught Latham's leader and knotted a big, bushy, overbuilt red and white thing onto the end of it. "I tie this for the backcountry," he said. "I call it the Rough-as-Guts Wulff. You can bang it around for years and it won't come apart."

Latham's first cast was short. On his second, the rainbow drifted up from the cress, followed the fly for a moment—perhaps pissed off, it was hard to tell—then ate it. And Hughie whooped.

Latham had hooked bigger trout on this trip, but none that

he fought as carefully. When it was nearly ready, Hughie made his way down the bank with his long-handled net, bringing up in me a rush of memories of other times with him on other rivers. Like a lot of us, he no longer moved as lightly as he once did, but he was laughing as he helped himself down through the brush, this Rough-as-Guts Hughie—his sun full out, hurrying toward a fish.

Latham flew back home to Auckland the following day, and Tom left on the morning after that. I met Geoffrey at Lake Tarawera, thirty minutes from Rotorua, on the morning Tom left so that we could drive back to Auckland together in Geoff's truck and end this road trip as we had all the others, singing together in a vehicle.

The Possum didn't look at all up for singing, though, when I got to John Donald's house on the lake around 8:00 A.M. An old mate of Geoff's, Donald is a retired farmer who now takes clients fishing and pig and deer hunting from his Tarawera home. He and Geoff and an undercover cop named Roger had partied hard all night long with a group of Aussie doctors after fishing the lake in the evening, and now—fourteen days after we had sallied out to catch the last blue cod in New Zealand— Geoff was a little pale around the gills and looked, for the first time, partied and road-tripped out. So we did what life has taught us to do for that and almost any other condition: we took a few beers in a cooler and went fishing. Roger and Geoff and I took Geoff's boat onto Lake Tarawera and threw streamers on sinking lines, unsuccessfully trying to tempt one of the big, zippy rainbows that live there into becoming Geoff's dinner that night back home in Auckland.

Almost a decade and a half ago, on my second trip to New Zealand, I had spent most of a day from dawn onward doing this with Geoff and Hughie McDowell. I was fairly new to

Kiwi keenness, and I remember marveling at how long and well and indefatigably the two of them cast the full sinking lines, and with what fervor they caught and killed the big lake fish. I was still astonished then at how hard the Kiwis went at their pleasures—drinking, laughing, hunting, and fishing harder and with less guilt and fastidiousness and fewer calls back to the wife or the office than anyone I had ever run into. It felt as footloose and unconstrained as living for outdoors pleasure felt when you were a boy. It felt to me like hunting or fishing with your grandfather when you were young and didn't know or care what a computer was or how the stock market was doing, and could give yourself wholly and without second thought to waters and fields that were replete and uncrowded and promised to stay that way forever.

The regal black swans with their white cygnets were still on the lake. The volcano still reared above it like a movie set. The brush, with its bellbirds and tuis, was still as thick and deep at the national park end of the lake as it was fourteen years ago, and the jade water as clear and cold. Geoffrey and I cast into it with concentration for about an hour, not needing a fish, and when we reeled in he had come right.

We put the boat on the trailer and an oldies tape on the deck, and pointed the Toyota north toward Auckland. The truck had been given to Thomas for promotion. The boat, full of promotional tackle, was replaced every year free of charge by a company also looking for promotion. In 1991, after the business we started together failed, and while I was picking up various pieces of my own life and trying to put those pieces together into something different, the Possum made a tape called "Snapper Secrets" that became the second-best-selling video in New Zealand history. Then he made "Kingfish

Secrets," "Shooting Secrets," "Surfcasting Secrets," "Seafood Secrets," "Trout Secrets," "Catch More Fish," "Bluewater Magic," "More Snapper Secrets," and tapes on bungie jumping, aerobics, cricket, and rugby. He got burned on some of the latter, nonfishing tapes and was now back to minding his knitting. He had six new tapes coming out in the next eighteen months, including "Snapper Secrets 3," and said he reckoned he might do a very short one called "Blue Cod Secrets," containing the following dramatized advice:

1. Put boat in water.
2. Put hook in sea.
3. Reel in cod.

He had a weekly column called "Gone Fishing" in the *New Zealand Herald*, the country's biggest daily; a weekly hour-long talk show called *Fishing and Outdoors* on the largest nationwide radio station; and he was developing a new outdoors show for TV New Zealand. He was also working on a series of fishing guides to follow the seven books he had already published, was a senior writer for Bob South's magazine, and was even doing some organizing of sporting side-travel for the sailing fat cats who would be coming into Auckland in 2000 for the America's Cup.

The Possum had been seriously scratching and hauling since the last time I saw him, and had even found the unspeakable energy and optimism to start a new family since then. He and his wife, Vicky, had recently added three children to the two now-grown ones they already had, one of whom has two children of her own older than Geoff's youngest.

But my man had managed to keep his priorities straight.

Like many another Kiwi, Thomas seems to live by all the maxims contained in this Chinese proverb at once, but to pay the most attention to the bottom line.

If you want to be joyous for one hour, get drunk.
If you want to be joyous for three days, get married.
If you want to be joyous for eight days, kill a pig and eat it.
If you want to be joyous forever, learn to fish.

Elvis was singing, "Are You Lonesome Tonight?" and we were warbling along.

"Well, where are we going next year?" Geoffrey asked when the song was over. "They're catching stripies by the bloody boatload out at the Three Kings Islands. And I'm in on this 1,800-acre multimillion-dollar game preserve ten minutes from Rotorua. Mate of mine is doing it. It's got two Scottish gamekeepers, pheasant, quail, ducks, trophy stags, pigs . . ." He head was bobbing a mile a minute. "Pointing dogs, retrievers, big trout in the ponds . . ."

"How about fishing the country around Waikaremoana?"

"Yehyehyeh!"

"And there's this valley I'd like to see again on the South Island."

"Yehyehyeh, we'll do it all, mate," said the Possum. "*Shitch*yeh!"

UNTIL I WAS OUT OF COLLEGE AND MARRIED, MY FATHER and I rarely got along anywhere but in a fishing boat. Mostly it was my fault that we didn't get along. I was not an easy kid to raise, particularly for a man who was almost forty when I was born, a perfectionist who was forced to spend his middle years wrestling both with himself and certain members of the family he had married into and felt, therefore, a little chapped about having gotten for an only son a kid with a six-foot wild hair up his rear end who needed wrestling, too.

My father was, back then, a man of strenuous and often debilitating appetites. In his forties he nearly died from a bleeding ulcer he got from the IRS and too much rich food. His own father died the color of a peach from booze, and so would my father have, had he not sometime in his fifties, finally and for good, won his twenty-year-long struggle with that particular appetite. His appetite for money and professional success, though it got him in the end most of what he wanted, was soured for a long time by the frustrations of putting his good mind and MIT engineering degree to work for those things within the stodgy, hierarchical family business he married into. In the years between when he retired at sixty-seven and when he died at eighty-three, his appetites ran mostly to electric sheets, tennis, Hawaiian Punch, warm weather, Belgian loafers, and travel. About the only hunger he had in common then with himself at fifty, or forty, or twenty, was for fishing—the one thing he could never get enough of in middle age that didn't disagree with him.

My father started me fishing for redfish in Florida before I was five, and he taught me to fly-fish before I was ten. By then we had moved from Florida to Birmingham, Alabama, and he was in full swing, wearing himself thin. He fished with buddies all over the world back then, for various reasons. At home, in home waters, I think he fished mostly to recover; for that, and to give himself and me time to get along.

I'd be in trouble in school. Or Bobby Carlson and Frank Young and I would have been seen running naked down the Mountain Brook Parkway, or caught shooting out street lamps with BB guns. My father would come home from the office, sit in his lounge chair in front of the TV and hear about it, still dressed in his suit pants and a button-down Brooks Brothers shirt, still looking avid from the day but worn down by it, too. He would sit and ponder whatever it was I had done, then get suddenly crisp around the mouth. My mother would ask that "it" wait until after dinner, which was served every evening at six-fifteen on the dot by a black man and woman with whom I was on much more intimate terms than I was with my father. "It" came about eight-thirty or nine o'clock, and consisted usually of a half-dozen measured strokes to my butt with a two-foot-long shoehorn. It never occurred to me then that my father was often spanking more than me. I believed then, and do now, that I usually deserved what I got and therefore I didn't understand until much later the gesture that sometimes followed the spankings. I'd be in bed, maybe asleep. He'd open the door to my room and stand there for a minute, backlit by the hall. "Son?" he'd say.

He'd walk into the room, sit on the side of my bed, and bend over and hug me, smelling of bourbon. Then, if it was spring or summer or fall, my father would say, "We'll go fishing on Saturday."

◆   ◆   ◆

The first home water I remember was at Louis Ford's ranch on the Black Warrior River near Tuscaloosa. Louis had for fishing water not only the river but a number of ponds and lakes full of bass, crappie, and big bluegills. We'd fish the lakes on the surface in the morning and late afternoons for bass, using Dalton Specials and a lure Louis said imitated a baby bird fallen out of a nest. In the middle of the day my father and I could take sardines and crackers and RC Colas down the slow, muddy river, and fill the boat with crappie and bluegills. Sometimes Louis would go with us on the river and tell stories while he fished— like about the time my father kept the boat from sinking when a stump tore a hole in the bow below the waterline and he patched it on the spot with a raincoat and screws he took out of an old wooden tackle box.

Louis was a big, red-faced, horn-handed countryman, and he and my father loved each other. One winter my father invited Louis up to a formal dance at a country club in Birmingham. Somehow, dressed in an unfamiliar tuxedo, Louis got his feelings hurt at the dance and drove himself and his beautiful wife home to Tuscaloosa. He and my father didn't see much of each other after that night. Louis died years later without either of them having put a patch to whatever happened at the party.

For a few years after Louis's place, our home water was a series of private bass lakes around Birmingham that belonged to friends and business associates of my father's. Some of those lakes were prettier or fishier than others, but every one of them gave my father pleasure and calm. If it was a weekday during the summer, he would come home from the office around two and we would fish until dark. If it was Saturday or Sunday, we would fish all day.

Before we actually got to the lake, on the car ride out or during the meticulous preparations we made together before we left, he could be thinking about things and irritable, his painstaking reaction to stress shunted for the time being into worrying the tackle, electric motor, batteries, and rain gear together, or into wondering if I had on enough clothes or had been to the bathroom. But once we reached the lake and he opened the door to one of his succession of yachtlike Buicks, stepped out, and looked at the water, he quit wrestling anything. It was time out for him, and he would come open like a fist unclenching. I could have broken into his liquor cabinet the night before, stolen a car, and driven through the lobby of the Alabama Theater, and all he'd have to say about it beside a bass lake the next day—grinning hungrily, grabbing the rods and the tackle box, and leaving me to bring the motor and batteries down—would be, "Come on, Skip. You can't catch fish with your worm out of water."

It didn't matter whether we caught fish or not, though we usually did—the entire time we were on the lake he was delighted and noisy. He would sit in the back running the electric motor, both of us fly-fishing a bank with yellow poppers. He would point out beaver signs and wild fruit trees, and instruct me on how to smell a bream bed and how to tell in my sinuses when low pressure was coming, and he would talk nonstop—about "Crunch and Des" stories, John Alden Knight, his youth—his voice so detached and unemphatic and continuous that you had the impression he was not so much talking as just scoring his fishing.

When I was thirteen my father bought his own lake near a place called Margaret about forty-five minutes from Birmingham. Lake Tadpole, as we called it, was home water to him until he died, and to me until I married and left Alabama. Tadpole was really two lakes, a small upper one and a twelve-acre lower one, set in a valley in the north Alabama hills. It was and is a beautiful place—the big lake a buxom, feminine shape ringed by dogwoods and fruit trees and old pines—and he and I believed it was as good a piece of bass water as there was in Alabama. But its real significance to me was as the place where my father and I went to get along after I ran away from one prep school and was kicked out of another; after his mother died; after I left college and hitchhiked around the country for a year working on mackerel boats and mango farms; and, after finally realizing I would never come to work for it, he sold the division of the family company that he had built from scratch.

After I was married, we still went there together to get along whenever I was in Birmingham, though getting along everywhere else was easier then. We continued to go out of habit, I suppose, and because we still enjoyed the perspective that being at the lake together in a fishing boat gave each of us on the other, the depth of field of hundreds of old afternoons of lenience with each other that it provided.

◆　　　◆　　　◆

I had Lough Corrib for home water in Ireland for two years, and didn't fish in Georgia. Dick Wentz and I shared a piece of fine home water called Rath's Pond in Iowa for a couple of years, then we both moved to Wisconsin and had a triangle of Lake Michigan and the creeks in Door County for three more. During those years my wife and I had three children and got graduate degrees. I made a living having fun, published a few stories and poems, and fished around a little in Canada, Mexico, and the Bahamas.

There was hardly anything to recover from during those seven years. Everybody got along beautifully, and it wasn't ever necessary to take bearings in order to get from one place to another. Home water, therefore, good as it was sometimes, didn't mean too much to me. In one gorgeous, fir-lined home creek in Door County, near the mouth of which Wentz and I, and only Wentz and I, would take perfectly colored two-pound brookies every September on deer-hair dry flies—I even rigged a fishing picture for a magazine. I hooked a long-dead ten-pound Lake Michigan steelhead to a streamer and let some guy photograph me netting it from the creek. When you can act like that and find it funny, you don't need home water.

What made me need it again was a coked-up, self-indulgent year of helping turn my first novel into a movie. That was twenty-five years ago now. Since then there has been more going to the mat with Hollywood, and with publishers and books, the travel business, mortgages, marriage, critics, and appetites; and there has been all the far-flung fishing I ever dreamed about. I am now closing in on sixty. I use a compass some of the time, and I would no more net a dead trout out of home water for a photographer than I would sell my bird dogs and move to Beverly Hills.

I have a daughter and two sons. Neither of those sons has ever shot out a street lamp or run naked down a highway, and I have never had to wrestle with either of them except for fun. The older one likes to fish, but the younger one loves it, and has since he was little, in the same indiscriminate, dreaming way that both my father and I did when we were kids. That younger son's name is Shelby, but we have always called him Judge.

When I got back to our home in New Hampshire after the movie debacle, skinny and psychically banged up, I fished nearly every afternoon of that July, and most days I took Judge along. Our home water then was a majestic three-mile stretch of the Contoocook River. Judge and I would put in the canoe around four in the afternoon and float until nearly dark. He hadn't learned to use a fly rod yet, so he would throw a spinner while I popped the banks and the rocks like a thirsty man drinking water. We caught a lot of smallmouths that month, and while we caught them, Judge would dream out loud about the sea-run brown trout and the bluefin tuna we would catch the following month when we went to Prince Edward Island. Those days in July that year were for me unspeakably sweet and restorative, complete in themselves without needed or wanted reference to any other thing or place. To Judge, six, with no need for any of the peculiar graces home water bestows, they were, well . . . the Contoocook River.

And so was our stretch of the Blackwater River—with its overgrown banks and still pools, its smart smallmouths and brown trout—only the Blackwater to Judge when it was home water, and we'd float it and he'd make me tell him about fishing for black marlin in Australia, even when he'd cast a hairmouse fly behind a drowned birch tree and watch the eddy come apart as a smallmouth crashed it.

Catching big wild brook trout in western Maine, sailfish off Stuart, Florida, and bluefish after bluefish over nineteen pounds off the Isles of Shoals made Judge, by the summer he was twelve, nearly permanently blasé about home water.

That August, a movie producer friend of ours came from California to New Hampshire for a four-day visit and brought his new wife and teenaged son and daughter. The boy was a little older than Judge and a lot higher-geared. He was dark, good-looking, and amusing. He could tell a Ferrari from a Maserati, and he knew Jack Nicholson. He also liked to fish. He had fished quite a bit in California and Florida with his father, but he had never caught a good bass, so Judge and I took him one afternoon to our home water.

That water then was a lake, one of the most beautiful I've ever seen, three miles from our house and virtually unfished except by my family. There were pickerel in this lake, bluegills, perch, and a lot of big bass, both largemouth and smallmouth. Judge and I had both caught four-to-five-pound bass there, and he had lost a largemouth that spring that would have gone over six. We fished for these bass with popping bugs, in the evening usually, and we always released them.

Well, we got to this lake, the producer's son, Judge, and I, around five o'clock, an hour and a half before the good top-water fishing started. Both Judge and I would rather catch one fish on top than five down deep, but the producer's son was after a big bass, so, after throwing a floating Rapala for a while with my spinning rod and noting that none of us were getting hits from good fish, he asked if he could put on a plastic worm.

I said sure.

"If you just wait," Judge told him, "until the water cools off, they'll start hitting that Rapala." Since he was sitting in the middle of the canoe, Judge was fishing with a spinning rod, too, using a frog popping plug.

The producer's son put on the worm and caught a couple of pound-and-a-half bass. He was thrilled with the fish, and I told him they were beauties. Judge just looked at them and kept throwing his frog. He shook his head when the producer's son said he wanted to keep the second bass. I told the kid we didn't usually keep the fish out of this lake. He looked disappointed and said he wanted to eat it, so I killed the bass for him.

Around six-thirty the sun went off the good bank, the breeze lay down, and the lake went totally still. Martens started to skim for insects. A pair of wood ducks flew over, whistling. And fish began to dimple the surface. A big pickerel took my popping bug, throwing up spray. I hit the fish and pulled back an empty leader.

"*Jesus,*" said the producer's son, looking at the place where the fish hit. "He was so big he broke off your fly."

"Snake," said Judge with disdain. "That was just a pickerel. He bit it off." Five minutes later he threw his frog up by a rock ten feet from shore and twitched it once. A three-pound largemouth hopped all over it. Judge smiled while he fought the fish, and when he released it he said, "Now *that's* a bass."

The producer's son watched the whole thing, from the splashy hit through the release, without saying anything. Then he took a few more casts with the worm, and asked Judge if he could try the frog.

"You're probably right," Judge told him. "You'll catch more fish with that worm."

We drove home in the dark and the producer's son asked if we could come back and fish the lake early the next morning. I told him I couldn't. There was a silence in the car. "You and Judge could fish, though," I said. More silence. "When you get home, make some sandwiches. I'll bring you guys out at five and you can fish until nine or so."

The next morning was foggy and still. I got the boys up at four-thirty and we left the house at five. Both boys were sleepy and grouchy and unhappy with the fog. When we got to the lake, I took the canoe off the Jeep and helped them load it. I asked Judge what he wanted for tackle. "I guess we'll just take the spinning rods," he said. His eyes were still half closed and he sounded bored. As I watched them carry the canoe down through the fog to the water, I thought it was likely to be a long morning for them out there.

I came back at nine-thirty and walked down to the lake. The canoe was just off the point of one of the three islands a hundred yards offshore. The producer's son was in the bow, casting to the point. Judge was in the stern, his paddle in his lap, and I could hear his voice. The lake was still perfectly calm. The fog had thinned a little without lifting, and it hung behind the canoe like a gray-white curtain. The islands, the canoe, the boys, and a dull silver patch of water between us were all there was to see.

I heard Judge laugh. Watching him in the stern, isolated on the water against the curtain of fog, I felt a quick surge of love for him rise and catch in my throat along with something I wanted to say so badly I almost shouted it out across the water. As it happened, I didn't even speak it, then or ever, because I didn't have to, and because I had learned on other lakes a long time before that the best lessons have little or nothing to do with words. But if I had, it would have gone like this: "This isn't just a place to wet a line, Judge. This is *home base*—where you start and what you come back to: the place that gives meaning and relevance to every other place you'll ever go."

"How're you doing?" I yelled.

They looked up and paddled in, taking their time. When they got close I could see they were doing fine. I beached the canoe and the producer's son got out. "Good morning?" I asked him.

"It was a *great* morning. Wasn't it, Judge?"

Judge grinned at me. "Jonathan caught some beauties on the frog."

"Keep any?"

"Nope. We released them," said Jonathan.

"How'd you do?" I asked Judge.

"Oh, not so good." He stood up and stretched, and gazed out over the water, looking proprietary and happy. "I fished the worm for a while . . . then I just had a good time watching Jon fish."